GERMAN CHRISTMAS MARKET GUIDE

The Ultimate Guide to Germany's Magical Holiday Markets: Best Cities, Festive Traditions, and Seasonal Delights

2024-2025 EDITION

Allan Richard

TABLE OF CONTENTS

PREFACE

As the first snowflakes begin to fall and the crisp winter air fills with the scent of roasted almonds and mulled wine, there's no place quite as magical as a German Christmas market. For me, it all started one frosty December evening in the heart of Munich. I was bundled up in a thick scarf, my hands wrapped around a steaming cup of Glühwein, and as I wandered through the festively lit stalls, I was transported into a world that seemed straight out of a storybook. The laughter of children, the twinkling lights reflecting off ornaments, and the warmth of the holiday spirit were palpable. It was in that moment that I realized how special these markets are—more than just places to shop; they are places where memories are made.

This guide is the culmination of years of exploration, not just of the markets themselves but of the traditions, stories, and local secrets that make each one unique. From the bustling market squares of Cologne and Nuremberg to the charming, lesser-known villages that dot the countryside, I've traveled far and wide to bring you the most comprehensive and delightful guide to Germany's Christmas markets.

But why a guide? Because there's something indescribable about the feeling you get when you first step into a German Christmas market. It's a blend of history, culture, and pure holiday joy that can't be found anywhere else in the world. I wanted to share that feeling with others—to help you not only find the best markets but to immerse yourself in the magic that they offer. Whether it's your first time visiting or you're a seasoned traveler, this guide is designed to bring the markets to life before you even set foot in Germany.

So, what can you expect from this guide? For starters, you'll find detailed descriptions of each market, including their unique features, must-try foods, and hidden gems that only locals know about. I'll take you on a journey through the history of these markets, explaining the traditions that have been passed down through generations. You'll learn how to navigate the markets like a pro, from understanding the local customs to finding the best time to visit.

But more than that, I hope this guide will inspire you to embrace the spirit of the season, to step away from the hustle and bustle of daily life, and to lose yourself in the wonder of a German Christmas market. Because in the end, it's not just about the places you visit; it's about the experiences you carry with you long after the last ornament is packed away.

Here's to your next adventure—one filled with joy, wonder, and the unforgettable charm of a German Christmas market.

INTRODUCTION TO GERMAN CHRISTMAS MARKETS

THE HISTORY OF CHRISTMAS MARKETS IN GERMANY

Germany's Christmas markets, known as *Weihnachtsmärkte,* are steeped in history, tracing their origins back to the late Middle Ages. These markets, which began as simple trading fairs, have since evolved into cherished holiday traditions celebrated not just across Germany, but around the world. Understanding the historical context of these markets offers insight into why they are so deeply ingrained in the cultural fabric of Germany today.

Medieval Beginnings: The Birth of a Tradition

The roots of Christmas markets can be traced back to the late 14th century, with one of the earliest recorded markets taking place in Bautzen, Saxony, in 1384. Originally, these markets were practical in nature, serving as winter fairs where townspeople could purchase food and supplies to last through the harsh winter months. Over time, these markets began to align with the Advent season, gradually taking on a more festive and celebratory atmosphere.

By the 15th century, Christmas markets had spread to many German cities, including Dresden, where the *Striezelmarkt* was first held in 1434. Named after a type of sweet bread (Stollen), this market is one of the oldest Christmas markets in the world and remains a popular destination to this day. These early markets featured not only food and goods but also entertainment, such as musical performances and puppet shows, helping to create a festive environment that drew in visitors from surrounding areas.

Evolution Through the Centuries: From Local Fairs to Cultural Phenomenons

As the centuries passed, Christmas markets grew in both size and significance. During the 16th and 17th centuries, the markets began to reflect the broader religious and cultural practices associated with the Christmas season. The Protestant Reformation, led by Martin Luther, played a significant role in shaping the markets, as Luther promoted the idea of giving gifts to children during the Christmas season. This tradition began to be reflected in the goods sold at the markets, with merchants offering handmade toys, sweets, and other gifts designed to delight children and celebrate the holiday spirit.

The 19th century brought further evolution as Germany underwent significant social and economic changes during the Industrial Revolution. Cities expanded, transportation improved, and more people were able to visit the markets. The markets themselves became more elaborate, with the addition of decorative stalls, Christmas trees, and more specialized holiday products, such as ornaments, candles, and nativity scenes. These markets began to symbolize not just the festive spirit of Christmas but also the communal values of togetherness and generosity.

By the early 20th century, the tradition of Christmas markets had become firmly established as an integral part of German holiday culture. Even during the turmoil of the World Wars, the markets persisted, providing a sense of continuity and hope amidst difficult times. After World War II, Christmas markets experienced a resurgence, particularly in West Germany, where they became symbols of cultural revival and economic recovery. The markets continued to grow in popularity, eventually spreading beyond Germany's borders to other parts of Europe and the world.

Christmas markets in Germany are more than just places to shop; they are cultural institutions that embody the spirit of the holiday season. These markets are deeply intertwined with German traditions, offering a glimpse into the country's rich cultural heritage. To understand the significance of these markets, it's essential to explore the customs, practices, and symbols that define them.

Advent: The Countdown to Christmas

Central to the cultural significance of German Christmas markets is the tradition of Advent, the period leading up to Christmas. Advent, derived from the Latin word *adventus* (meaning "coming"), is a time of anticipation and preparation for the celebration of the birth of Christ. The markets traditionally open during the first week of Advent, marking the beginning of the holiday season.

Advent calendars, which originated in Germany in the 19th century, are a popular way to count down the days until

Christmas. These calendars often feature little doors or windows that open to reveal a small treat or image, symbolizing the joy and anticipation of the season. At Christmas markets, you'll find a wide variety of Advent calendars, from simple paper versions to elaborate wooden ones, often crafted with intricate detail.

Another key symbol of Advent is the Advent wreath, or *Adventskranz*. Traditionally, this wreath is made of evergreen branches and adorned with four candles, each representing one of the four Sundays leading up to Christmas. Every Sunday, a new candle is lit, symbolizing the growing light as Christmas approaches. These wreaths are often sold at Christmas markets and are a common sight in German homes and churches during the holiday season.

Traditional Foods and Drinks: A Feast for the Senses

No visit to a German Christmas market would be complete without indulging in the traditional foods and drinks that are synonymous with the season. These culinary delights not only satisfy the taste buds but also carry deep cultural significance, reflecting regional variations and centuries-old recipes.

One of the most iconic treats is *Lebkuchen*, a type of spiced gingerbread that dates back to the Middle Ages. Originally made by monks in Franconia, *Lebkuchen* comes in various forms, from soft, cake-like cookies to harder, more biscuit-like versions. These gingerbreads are often shaped into hearts, stars, or other festive designs and decorated with icing and nuts. At Christmas markets, *Lebkuchen* is often sold in decorative tins or wrapped in colorful packaging, making it a popular gift.

Glühwein is another staple of the Christmas market experience. This warm, spiced wine is typically made with red wine, cinnamon, cloves, and citrus, and is served steaming hot to ward off the winter chill. The origins of *Glühwein* can be traced back to the medieval period, and it remains a beloved tradition today. Visitors to the markets can often find variations of *Glühwein*, including white wine versions and non-alcoholic alternatives like *Kinderpunsch*.

Other traditional foods include *Stollen*, a dense fruitcake coated in powdered sugar, and *Bratwurst*, grilled sausages often served with mustard in a bun. Regional specialties also abound, such as *Schneeballen* (deep-fried dough balls from Bavaria) and *Baumkuchen* (a layered cake from Saxony). These foods not only provide nourishment but also serve as a way to connect with Germany's culinary heritage.

Craftsmanship and Gifts: A Celebration of Artisanship

German Christmas markets are renowned for their emphasis on traditional craftsmanship. Many of the goods sold at these markets are handmade by local artisans, making each item unique and imbued with a sense of history and tradition. From delicate glass ornaments to intricately carved wooden figurines, the craftsmanship on display at these markets is a testament to Germany's rich artisanal heritage.

Wooden toys and decorations, such as *Räuchermännchen* (smoking figures) and *Weihnachtspyramiden* (Christmas pyramids), are particularly popular. These items are often handcrafted in the Erzgebirge region, known for its long tradition of wood carving. The *Räuchermännchen,* typically depicting a figure holding a pipe, doubles as an incense burner, filling the air with the scent of Christmas spices. The *Weihnachtspyramiden* are multi-tiered structures adorned with candles, figurines, and a central propeller that spins when the candles are lit, creating a mesmerizing display.

Glassblowing is another traditional craft showcased at Christmas markets. The town of Lauscha, in the Thuringian Forest, is famous for its glass ornaments, which have been produced there since the 16th century. These delicate ornaments, often hand-painted and adorned with glitter, are a quintessential part of German Christmas decorations and are prized by collectors around the world.

In addition to traditional crafts, many markets feature stalls selling contemporary gifts, such as jewelry, clothing, and art. However, even these modern offerings often reflect the same commitment to quality and craftsmanship that defines the more traditional goods. For many visitors, purchasing a handcrafted item at a Christmas market is not just about acquiring a souvenir; it's about taking home a piece of German culture and tradition.

WHY GERMANY IS THE ULTIMATE CHRISTMAS MARKET DESTINATION

Germany is widely regarded as the ultimate destination for Christmas markets, and it's easy to see why. The country's markets are unparalleled in their variety, atmosphere, and authenticity, offering a holiday experience that is truly magical. But what sets German Christmas markets apart from those in other countries? To answer this question, we must delve into the elements that make these markets unique.

Atmosphere: A Blend of History and Holiday Cheer

One of the most distinctive features of German Christmas markets is their atmosphere. Each market, whether large or small, is infused with a sense of history and tradition that creates an enchanting holiday ambiance. Many of the markets are set against the backdrop of historic town squares, medieval castles, or grand cathedrals, adding to the sense of timelessness and wonder.

The markets are meticulously decorated, with twinkling lights, garlands of evergreen, and festive ornaments adorning the stalls and surrounding buildings. The air is filled with the sounds of holiday music, from traditional carols to live performances by local choirs and bands. The scent of *Glühwein,* roasted chestnuts, and gingerbread wafts through the air, tantalizing the senses and inviting visitors to indulge in the delights of the season.

But it's not just the physical setting that creates the magical atmosphere; it's also the sense of community and togetherness that pervades the markets. These markets are places where people come together to celebrate the season, whether it's sharing a meal with friends, finding the perfect gift for a loved one, or simply enjoying the festive spirit. This sense of camaraderie and joy is palpable, making every visit to a German Christmas market a heartwarming experience.

Variety: A Market for Every Taste

Another factor that sets German Christmas markets apart is the sheer variety they offer. Germany is home to hundreds of Christmas markets, each with its own unique character and charm. From the large, internationally renowned markets like those in Nuremberg and Cologne to the small, intimate markets in rural villages, there is something for everyone.

For those seeking a traditional experience, markets like Nuremberg's *Christkindlesmarkt* offer a classic blend of history, craftsmanship, and holiday cheer. This market, one of the oldest and most famous in Germany, features over 180 stalls selling everything from handcrafted ornaments to local delicacies. The market is also known for its *Christkind*, a young woman who, dressed in angelic attire, opens the market with a festive prologue and spreads holiday cheer to visitors.

For those looking for something a bit different, markets like the *Mittelaltermarkt* in Esslingen offer a unique twist on the traditional Christmas market. This market, set in the medieval town of Esslingen, recreates the atmosphere of a medieval market, complete with costumed vendors, traditional crafts, and entertainment like jousting and fire shows. It's an immersive experience that transports visitors back in time while still capturing the magic of the holiday season.

In addition to traditional and themed markets, Germany also offers specialized markets, such as the *Reiterlesmarkt* in Rothenburg ob der Tauber, known for its beautifully preserved medieval architecture, or the Maritime Christmas Market in Lübeck, which celebrates the city's Hanseatic heritage with nautical-themed decorations and offerings. Whether you're interested in history, culture, or simply enjoying the festive spirit, you'll find a market that suits your tastes in Germany.

Authenticity: A True Reflection of German Culture

Perhaps the most compelling reason why Germany is the ultimate Christmas market destination is the authenticity of its markets. Unlike some holiday markets that have become overly commercialized, German Christmas markets remain deeply rooted in tradition and culture. The emphasis on local craftsmanship, regional specialties, and traditional customs ensures that visitors experience a true reflection of German holiday culture.

This authenticity is evident in the goods sold at the markets, which often include handmade items created by local artisans. Whether it's a carved wooden figure from the Erzgebirge, a hand-blown glass ornament from Lauscha, or a piece of traditional *Lebkuchen* from Nuremberg, each item carries with it a sense of history and tradition. These markets are not just places to shop; they are places to connect with the cultural heritage of Germany.

Moreover, the authenticity of German Christmas markets is also reflected in the way they are celebrated by the local communities. These markets are not just tourist attractions; they are an integral part of the holiday season for many Germans. Families, friends, and neighbors come together to visit the markets, participate in the festivities, and celebrate the traditions that have been passed down through generations. This sense of continuity and cultural pride is what makes German Christmas markets so special.

Accessibility: A Welcoming Destination for All Travelers

Finally, Germany's Christmas markets are renowned for their accessibility and inclusivity, making them a welcoming destination for travelers from around the world. Whether you're a solo traveler, a couple, a family with children, or a group of friends, you'll find that the markets offer something for everyone.

Many of the larger markets, such as those in Berlin, Munich, and Frankfurt, are easily accessible by public transportation, making it convenient to visit multiple markets in a single trip. Additionally, many markets offer family-friendly activities, such as carousels, ice skating rinks, and Santa Claus visits, ensuring that visitors of all ages can enjoy the festive spirit.

For international travelers, Germany's reputation for hospitality and its robust tourism infrastructure make it an ideal destination for a holiday getaway. English is widely spoken, particularly in the larger cities and tourist areas, and many markets offer information and services in multiple languages. This welcoming atmosphere, combined with the enchanting beauty of the markets, makes Germany an unparalleled destination for experiencing the magic of Christmas.

German Christmas markets are more than just holiday shopping destinations; they are cultural institutions that embody the spirit of the season. From their medieval origins to their modern-day celebrations, these markets offer a unique blend of history, tradition, and festive cheer. Whether you're drawn by the allure of handcrafted gifts, the warmth of a cup of *Glühwein*, or the joy of celebrating with loved ones, Germany's Christmas markets offer an experience like no other. As the ultimate Christmas market destination, Germany invites travelers from around the world to step into a winter wonderland and create memories that will last a lifetime.

TOP CHRISTMAS MARKETS ACROSS GERMANY

BERLIN: A CAPITAL OF HOLIDAY SPLENDOR

Berlin, Germany's vibrant capital, transforms into a winter wonderland each year, boasting over 80 Christmas markets scattered throughout the city. Each market has its own unique charm, offering visitors a delightful blend of history, culture, and festive cheer. Berlin's Christmas markets stand out not just for their number, but for their diversity—ranging from traditional to contemporary, from small and cozy to grand and bustling.

One of the most iconic markets is the Gendarmenmarkt Christmas Market, nestled between the German and French Cathedrals. This market is known for its stunning architecture, featuring elegantly decorated stalls surrounded by historic buildings. The Gendarmenmarkt is a feast for the senses, with artisan crafts, mouthwatering treats like bratwurst and roasted nuts, and live entertainment ranging from classical choirs to acrobatic performances. A large, glittering Christmas tree stands at the center, creating a picture-perfect scene that captures the essence of Berlin during the holidays.

Another must-see is the Charlottenburg Palace Christmas Market. Located in front of the magnificent baroque palace, this market is a visual spectacle, with the palace illuminated in festive colors, adding to the market's magical atmosphere. Here, visitors can enjoy a more serene experience, strolling through stalls offering handmade crafts, ornaments, and gourmet foods. The aroma of mulled wine fills the air, inviting guests to warm up with a glass while admiring the historic surroundings.

For those seeking something a bit more contemporary, the Berliner Weihnachtszeit at Roten Rathaus is a great choice. This market combines traditional charm with modern attractions, including a large ice-skating rink that circles around the Neptune Fountain, offering a fun activity for both children and adults. The market also features a historic Ferris wheel, providing panoramic views of the city's twinkling lights.

Berlin's Christmas markets are not just about shopping and food; they are cultural experiences that reflect the city's rich history and diversity. From the historic charm of the Gendarmenmarkt to the modern flair of Roten Rathaus, Berlin offers something for every holiday traveler. The city's markets are also conveniently connected by public transport, making it easy to explore multiple markets in one visit.

In Berlin, Christmas isn't just a holiday; it's a season-long celebration where tradition meets innovation, creating a festive atmosphere that captivates locals and visitors alike.

NUREMBERG: THE HISTORIC CHRISTKINDLESMARKT

Nuremberg's Christkindlesmarkt is one of the oldest and most famous Christmas markets in the world, dating back to the 16th century. This historic market, located in the heart of the city's Old Town, is a must-visit for anyone looking to experience the quintessential German Christmas.

The market is officially opened each year by the Christkind, a young woman chosen to represent the spirit of Christmas. Dressed in a golden crown and white robe, she recites the traditional prologue from the balcony of the Frauenkirche, welcoming visitors to the market. This ceremony is deeply rooted in Nuremberg's culture and is one of the most anticipated events of the holiday season.

The Christkindlesmarkt is known for its traditional stalls, each offering a variety of handcrafted goods, from wooden toys and ornaments to intricate nativity scenes. A stroll through the market reveals a world of craftsmanship, with many items still made using techniques passed down through generations. The market's distinctive red-and-white striped stalls add to its old-world charm, creating a festive atmosphere that feels timeless.

One of the most iconic treats at the Christkindlesmarkt is Nuremberg Lebkuchen, a type of gingerbread that has been a local specialty for over 600 years. These spiced cookies, often decorated with icing or dipped in chocolate, make for a perfect holiday snack or souvenir. Another culinary highlight is the Nuremberger Rostbratwurst, small sausages served in a bun with mustard, offering a savory taste of the region's culinary heritage.

Beyond the market itself, Nuremberg offers a variety of festive events and attractions during the holiday season. The Kinderweihnacht, a market specifically designed for children, features a nostalgic carousel, a miniature Ferris wheel, and workshops where kids can decorate cookies or make their own crafts. There's also the Sternenhaus, a venue offering Christmas-themed performances, including puppet shows and concerts, adding to the city's festive offerings.

The Christkindlesmarkt is not just a market; it's a celebration of Nuremberg's history, culture, and community. Its enduring traditions and enchanting atmosphere make it one of the most beloved Christmas markets in Germany, drawing visitors from around the world to experience its unique blend of holiday cheer and historic charm.

MUNICH: FESTIVITIES IN BAVARIA

Munich's Christmas markets are a reflection of Bavaria's rich cultural traditions and festive spirit. The city's main market, the Christkindlmarkt at Marienplatz, is set against the backdrop of the stunning Neues Rathaus (New Town Hall), which is beautifully illuminated during the holiday season. This market is one of the oldest in Germany, with roots tracing back to the 14th century, and it remains a central part of Munich's Christmas celebrations.

The Christkindlmarkt is a vibrant hub of activity, with over 150 stalls offering everything from handcrafted ornaments and traditional Bavarian gifts to delicious seasonal treats. The aroma of freshly baked Stollen (a fruitcake filled with marzipan) and sizzling Bratwurst fills the air, tempting visitors to indulge in the market's culinary delights. One of the market's highlights is the Kripperlmarkt, dedicated to nativity scenes. Here, you can find everything needed to create a traditional Bavarian nativity, from hand-carved figures to ornate mangers.

Bavarian traditions are evident throughout Munich's Christmas markets. For example, the Feuerzangenbowle, a popular hot drink made by setting a rum-soaked sugarloaf on fire and letting it drip into mulled wine, is a must-try. This warm, spiced beverage is perfect for warding off the winter chill and is a favorite among locals and visitors alike.

Another unique aspect of Munich's Christmas markets is the Tollwood Winter Festival, held at Theresienwiese, the same grounds as Oktoberfest. Tollwood offers a more contemporary take on the traditional Christmas market, with a focus on sustainability and world cultures. The festival features an eclectic mix of international foods, handmade crafts, and live performances, from music and theater to circus acts. Tollwood's vibrant atmosphere and diverse offerings make it a popular destination for those looking to experience a different side of Munich's holiday celebrations.

Munich's markets are also known for their festive activities. The Christmas Tram, a vintage tram decorated for the holidays, offers a cozy ride through the city while passengers enjoy mulled wine and gingerbread. The city's ice rinks, including the one at Karlsplatz, are also popular spots for both locals and tourists, providing a fun and festive way to enjoy the winter season.

In Munich, the Christmas markets are more than just a place to shop; they are a celebration of Bavarian culture and traditions, offering a warm and welcoming atmosphere that embodies the spirit of the season.

COLOGNE: THE MARKETS BY THE CATHEDRAL

Cologne's Christmas markets are among the most picturesque in Germany, and the markets by the Cologne Cathedral are the crown jewels. The Weihnachtsmarkt am Kölner Dom (Christmas Market at Cologne Cathedral) is set against the stunning backdrop of the UNESCO World Heritage-listed Gothic cathedral, one of the most iconic landmarks in Germany. This market is not only one of the largest in the country, but also one of the most beautiful, attracting millions of visitors each year.

The centerpiece of the market is a towering Christmas tree, one of the largest in the Rhineland, adorned with thousands of lights that cast a warm glow over the entire market. Around the tree, over 150 stalls offer a wide variety of goods, from handcrafted ornaments and wooden toys to gourmet chocolates and regional delicacies. The market's unique location, with the cathedral's spires rising majestically above, creates an awe-inspiring atmosphere that is hard to match.

One of the standout features of the Cologne Cathedral market is its commitment to quality and tradition. Many of the stalls are operated by local artisans who use traditional techniques to create their goods. Visitors can watch glassblowers, woodcarvers, and blacksmiths at work, adding an educational element to the shopping experience. The market also has a strong focus on sustainability, with eco-friendly products and initiatives aimed at reducing waste.

Cologne's Christmas markets are known for their festive entertainment, and the Cathedral market is no exception. Daily performances on the central stage feature choirs, bands, and dance groups, filling the air with holiday music and adding to the joyful atmosphere. For families, the market offers a variety of activities, including a children's carousel and a special workshop where kids can make their own Christmas crafts.

In addition to the Cathedral market, Cologne is home to several other notable markets, each with its own unique character. The Alter Markt in the Old Town is particularly charming, with its medieval-inspired stalls and a festive ice rink. The Heimat der Heinzel market, also in the Old Town, is inspired by the city's folklore and features a whimsical theme with gnome-like figures (Heinzelmännchen) hidden throughout the market.

Cologne's Christmas markets are more than just a shopping destination; they are an integral part of the city's cultural fabric. The combination of the stunning cathedral backdrop, the high-quality goods, and the festive atmosphere make these markets a must-visit for anyone seeking a truly magical holiday experience.

DRESDEN: THE STRIEZELMARKT EXPERIENCE

Dresden's Striezelmarkt is one of Germany's oldest Christmas markets, with a history dating back to 1434. Located in the city's Altmarkt Square, the Striezelmarkt is a celebration of Saxon traditions and one of the most authentic Christmas experiences in Germany. The market's name is derived from "Striezel," an old word for the famous Dresdner Stollen, a fruit-filled bread that has become synonymous with the holiday season.

The Striezelmarkt is a feast for the senses, with over 200 festively decorated stalls offering a wide array of goods, from handmade crafts and ornaments to local delicacies. The market is particularly known for its traditional Erzgebirge (Ore Mountains) folk art, including hand-carved wooden figures, Christmas pyramids, and Schwibbogen candle arches. These items, often intricately detailed and made with great care, make for unique and meaningful souvenirs.

One of the most iconic features of the Striezelmarkt is the world's tallest Christmas pyramid, a towering, multi-tiered wooden structure adorned with lights and rotating figures. This pyramid is a symbol of the market and a popular spot for visitors to take photos. The market also features a giant advent calendar displayed on one of the historic buildings surrounding the square, with a new window opened each day to reveal a festive scene.

The Striezelmarkt is deeply rooted in Dresden's culture, and its history is celebrated throughout the market. Visitors can learn about the market's origins and the traditions that have been passed down through centuries at the Dresdner Stollenfest, a special event held each December. During this festival, a giant Stollen is paraded through the streets of Dresden before being ceremoniously sliced and shared with the crowd. The Stollenfest is a highlight of the holiday season and offers a unique glimpse into the city's culinary heritage.

For families, the Striezelmarkt offers a variety of activities, including a children's area with a carousel, puppet theater, and a bakery where kids can decorate their own gingerbread cookies. The market also features live performances, from choirs and brass bands to traditional folk dancing, adding to the festive atmosphere.

The Striezelmarkt's combination of history, tradition, and festive cheer makes it one of the most beloved Christmas markets in Germany. Its authentic Saxon character and warm, welcoming atmosphere make it a must-visit destination for anyone looking to experience the true spirit of a German Christmas.

HAMBURG: A MARITIME CHRISTMAS MARKET

Hamburg's Christmas markets offer a unique blend of traditional holiday cheer and maritime charm, reflecting the city's rich history as one of Europe's major port cities. The markets are spread throughout the city, each with its own distinct atmosphere, but it is the Historic Christmas Market at the Town Hall that stands out as the centerpiece of Hamburg's festive celebrations.

The Town Hall market is set against the backdrop of the impressive neo-Renaissance Rathaus, which is beautifully illuminated during the holiday season. The market is designed to evoke the feeling of an old-world village, with rows of wooden stalls selling handcrafted goods, toys, and holiday treats. The market is particularly known for its focus on quality, with many of the goods being produced by artisans from across Germany.

What sets Hamburg's Christmas markets apart is their strong connection to the city's maritime heritage. The Weihnachtsmarkt auf dem Fleetinsel, located along the canals, offers a more intimate and serene experience. Here, visitors can enjoy the sight of festively decorated boats and stalls offering seafood delicacies, mulled wine, and maritime-themed gifts. The Fleetinsel market's unique setting, with the gentle lapping of the water and the glow of the lights reflecting on the canals, creates a magical atmosphere that is quintessentially Hamburg.

Another popular market is the Santa Pauli Christmas Market, located in the city's famous Reeperbahn district.

Known as Hamburg's "naughtiest" Christmas market, Santa Pauli offers a more adult-oriented take on the holiday season, with live music, burlesque shows, and stalls selling cheeky gifts. Despite its risqué reputation, Santa Pauli retains a festive atmosphere and has become a beloved part of Hamburg's holiday celebrations.

For those looking for a family-friendly experience, the Winterwald market at the St. Pauli Stadium offers a cozy, forest-themed setting with activities for children, including a mini-ice rink and a petting zoo. The market's rustic wooden huts and the scent of pine create a winter wonderland that delights visitors of all ages.

Hamburg's Christmas markets are a reflection of the city's vibrant and diverse character. Whether you're exploring the historic Town Hall market, enjoying the maritime ambiance of Fleetinsel, or experiencing the quirky charm of Santa Pauli, Hamburg offers a Christmas market experience that is as unique as the city itself.

STUTTGART: A CITY OF MARKETS AND FESTIVE CHEER

Stuttgart is home to one of Germany's largest and most beautifully decorated Christmas markets, drawing visitors from near and far to experience its festive charm. The Stuttgarter Weihnachtsmarkt is spread across several squares in the city center, with over 280 stalls offering a wide variety of goods, from handcrafted gifts and ornaments to delicious holiday treats. The market's picturesque setting, framed by historic buildings and the towering Stiftskirche, adds to its appeal, creating a festive atmosphere that is both lively and welcoming.

One of the most distinctive features of Stuttgart's Christmas market is the ornately decorated rooftops of the stalls. Each stallholder takes great pride in adorning their rooftop with elaborate displays, often featuring Christmas scenes, lights, and greenery. These decorations are a highlight of the market, drawing visitors to admire the creativity and effort put into making each stall a visual delight.

The market also has a strong focus on local traditions and craftsmanship. The Swabian crafts on display range from woodcarvings and pottery to textiles and jewelry, providing visitors with a wide selection of unique and high-quality gifts. Stuttgart's culinary offerings are equally impressive, with local specialties like Maultaschen (Swabian dumplings) and Schupfnudeln (potato noodles) taking center stage alongside more traditional holiday treats like roasted chestnuts and spiced wine.

In addition to the main market, Stuttgart hosts several smaller, themed markets that add to the city's festive appeal. The Finnish Christmas Village at the Karlsplatz, for example, offers a taste of Nordic holiday traditions, with stalls selling Finnish delicacies like reindeer sausage and Glögi (Finnish mulled wine), as well as handmade crafts from Finland. The Antique Market at Schillerplatz is another highlight, featuring a selection of vintage and antique goods that make for one-of-a-kind holiday gifts.

Stuttgart's Christmas markets are also known for their festive activities and entertainment. The Advent Concerts held in the Stiftskirche provide a beautiful backdrop of music to the market, while the Fairy Tale Land in the courtyard of the Old Castle offers a magical experience for children, with puppet shows, storytelling, and a miniature train.

The combination of stunning decorations, local craftsmanship, and festive activities makes Stuttgart's Christmas markets a standout destination during the holiday season. The city's warm and welcoming atmosphere, coupled with its rich cultural traditions, ensures that visitors will leave with memories of a truly enchanting Christmas experience.

This chapter has explored some of the top Christmas markets across Germany, each offering its own unique blend of history, tradition, and festive cheer. From the historic Christkindlesmarkt in Nuremberg to the maritime charm of Hamburg's Fleetinsel, Germany's Christmas markets are a testament to the country's rich cultural heritage and its love of the holiday season. Whether you're looking for traditional crafts, delicious food, or simply a warm and festive atmosphere, these markets offer something for everyone, making them must-visit destinations for any traveler during the Christmas season.

CHRISTMAS MARKET FOODS AND DRINKS

The aroma of sizzling sausages, freshly baked gingerbread, and spiced wine fills the air as you step into a German Christmas market. The food and drink offerings are a vital part of the Christmas market experience, providing a taste of traditional German holiday fare that's as rich in history as it is in flavor. In this chapter, we'll explore the must-try dishes and drinks, the stories behind them, and where to find the best food stalls in each market. Whether you're a foodie eager to savor every bite or simply looking to indulge in the festive spirit, this guide will lead you to the heart of Germany's culinary Christmas traditions.

MUST-TRY TRADITIONAL GERMAN HOLIDAY DISHES

1. Bratwurst: One of the most iconic foods at German Christmas markets is the bratwurst, a type of German sausage made from pork, beef, or veal. Traditionally grilled over an open flame, the bratwurst is served in a bun and topped with mustard or sauerkraut. The smoky, savory flavor of the bratwurst is a perfect match for the cold winter air, making it a must-try dish.

The significance of the bratwurst dates back centuries, with each region in Germany having its own variation of the sausage. For example, in Nuremberg, the Nürnberger Rostbratwurst is a smaller, more delicately spiced sausage, often served in groups of three on a roll. In Thuringia, the

Thüringer Rostbratwurst is known for its distinctive flavor, seasoned with marjoram, garlic, and caraway seeds.

2. Kartoffelpuffer: Another beloved Christmas market dish is the Kartoffelpuffer, or potato pancakes. These crispy, golden-brown patties are made from grated potatoes, onions, eggs, and flour, and are typically fried to perfection. They are often served with a dollop of applesauce or sour cream, providing a delightful contrast between the savory pancake and the sweet or tangy topping.

Kartoffelpuffer have their roots in the rural cuisine of Germany, where they were a simple yet hearty meal for farmers. Today, they are a staple at Christmas markets, offering a warm and comforting snack to enjoy as you stroll through the festive stalls.

3. Sauerkraut: Sauerkraut, or fermented cabbage, is a quintessential German dish that often accompanies sausages and other meats at Christmas markets. The tangy, slightly sour flavor of sauerkraut pairs beautifully with the

rich, savory flavors of traditional German dishes, making it a popular side dish.

Sauerkraut has a long history in German cuisine, dating back to ancient times when it was used as a method of preserving cabbage through the winter months. It is also known for its health benefits, as the fermentation process creates probiotics that are good for digestion.

4. Schupfnudeln: Schupfnudeln are a type of German dumpling or thick noodle made from potatoes and flour. They are often pan-fried and served with sauerkraut, bacon, or mushrooms. The chewy texture and savory flavor of Schupfnudeln make them a hearty and satisfying dish, perfect for warming up on a cold winter evening.

The origins of Schupfnudeln can be traced back to the Swabian region of Germany, where they were traditionally made as a way to use up leftover potatoes. Today, they are a popular street food at Christmas markets, offering a taste of rustic German comfort food.

GLÜHWEIN: THE WARM SPICED WINE OF WINTER

No visit to a German Christmas market is complete without a steaming mug of Glühwein, the quintessential winter beverage. Glühwein is a type of mulled wine made by heating red wine with a blend of spices, citrus, and sugar. The result is a fragrant, warming drink that is both soothing and invigorating.

How Glühwein is Made:

To make Glühwein, red wine is gently heated with a mixture of spices, such as cinnamon sticks, cloves, star anise, and nutmeg. Slices of oranges or lemons are often added for a hint of citrusy brightness, and sugar or honey is used to sweeten the wine to taste. The key is to heat the wine slowly, allowing the flavors to meld together without boiling off the alcohol.

Some variations of Glühwein include the addition of spirits, such as rum or brandy, for an extra kick. In some regions, you'll also find white wine versions of Glühwein, which are equally delicious and offer a slightly lighter, more refreshing option.

Why Glühwein is a Staple at Christmas Markets:
The tradition of drinking spiced wine during the winter months dates back to the Roman Empire, but it was in Germany that the practice truly became associated with the Christmas season. The warmth and spice of Glühwein make it the perfect antidote to the chilly winter weather, and its popularity has only grown over the centuries.

At Christmas markets, Glühwein is typically served in festive mugs that you can take home as a souvenir. Each market often has its own unique mug design, making it a fun and collectible memento of your visit.

Tips for Finding the Best Glühwein:
While you'll find Glühwein at nearly every Christmas market in Germany, not all mugs are created equal. To find the best Glühwein, look for stalls that make their own

blend from scratch rather than using pre-made mixes. You can often spot these stalls by the fragrant aroma of freshly brewed spices wafting through the air.

If you're visiting a market in a wine-producing region, such as the Rhineland or Franconia, be sure to try the local Glühwein, which may be made with regionally produced wines. Additionally, keep an eye out for stalls offering special variations, such as cherry Glühwein or apple-cinnamon Glühwein, for a unique twist on the classic drink.

SWEETS AND TREATS: GINGERBREAD, STOLLEN, AND MORE

German Christmas markets are a paradise for those with a sweet tooth, offering a wide array of traditional holiday treats that are as delicious as they are festive. Among the most iconic are gingerbread, Stollen, and a variety of cookies and pastries that have been enjoyed for generations.

1. Lebkuchen (Gingerbread): Lebkuchen, or German gingerbread, is a beloved Christmas treat that comes in

many shapes and forms. Unlike the crisp gingerbread cookies often found in other countries, Lebkuchen is typically soft and chewy, made with honey, spices, nuts, and sometimes fruit. The dough is often flavored with a blend of cinnamon, cloves, ginger, cardamom, and anise, giving it a warm, spicy aroma that is synonymous with the holiday season.

Lebkuchen is deeply rooted in German history, with some of the earliest recipes dating back to the Middle Ages. The city of Nuremberg is particularly famous for its Lebkuchen, where it has been produced by local bakers for over 600 years. Nuremberg Lebkuchen is often regarded as the finest, made with high-quality ingredients and crafted with care.

At Christmas markets, you'll find Lebkuchen in various forms, from simple round cookies to elaborately decorated hearts inscribed with festive messages. Some are coated in chocolate or glazed with icing, while others are left plain to showcase the rich flavors of the dough.

2. Christstollen: Christstollen, commonly known simply as Stollen, is a traditional German Christmas bread that is rich with dried fruits, nuts, and spices. The dough is often flavored with rum or brandy, and the finished loaf is dusted with powdered sugar to resemble the snow-covered landscapes of winter.

Stollen has its origins in Dresden, where it was first baked over 500 years ago. The bread was originally a simple, austere loaf made during the Advent season, but over time it evolved into the rich, buttery treat we know today. Dresden Stollen, or Dresdner Christstollen, is protected by a special designation, ensuring that only Stollen made in the city according to traditional methods can bear the name.

Each Christmas market will have its own version of Stollen, with variations in the types of fruits and nuts used. Whether you prefer a classic fruit Stollen or a more modern version with marzipan or chocolate, this sweet bread is a must-try during the holiday season.

3. Gebrannte Mandeln (Candied Almonds): The smell of roasting nuts is one of the most evocative scents at a German Christmas market. Gebrannte Mandeln, or candied almonds, are a popular treat, made by coating almonds in a mixture of sugar, cinnamon, and vanilla, and then roasting them until they are caramelized and crispy.

Gebrannte Mandeln are typically sold in paper cones, making them a convenient snack to enjoy as you wander through the market. The combination of sweet, crunchy almonds and the warmth of the cinnamon and vanilla makes this a truly irresistible treat.

4. Vanillekipferl: Vanillekipferl are delicate, crescent-shaped cookies flavored with vanilla and coated in powdered sugar. These buttery cookies are a staple of German holiday baking, and their melt-in-your-mouth texture makes them a favorite at Christmas markets.

The origins of Vanillekipferl can be traced to Austria, but they have become popular throughout Germany as well. They are often made with ground almonds or hazelnuts, which give the cookies a rich, nutty flavor that pairs perfectly with the sweet vanilla.

5. Spekulatius: Spekulatius are spiced shortcrust biscuits, traditionally baked in the shape of St. Nicholas or other festive figures. The dough is flavored with a blend of spices, including cinnamon, nutmeg, cloves, and cardamom, which give the cookies their distinctive taste.

These cookies are often associated with the Sinterklaas celebration in the Netherlands, but they are also a popular treat in Germany during the Christmas season. The intricate designs on Spekulatius cookies are created using carved wooden molds, making them as beautiful to look at as they are delicious to eat.

Recipes for Popular Treats:

Lebkuchen Recipe:
- Ingredients:
  - 3 cups all-purpose flour
  - 1 1/2 teaspoons baking powder

- 1/2 teaspoon baking soda

- 1 tablespoon ground cinnamon

- 1 teaspoon ground ginger

- 1/2 teaspoon ground cloves

- 1/2 teaspoon ground nutmeg

- 1/2 teaspoon ground cardamom

- 1/2 teaspoon ground anise

- 1/2 teaspoon salt

- 1/2 cup unsalted butter, softened

- 1 cup brown sugar, packed

- 1/2 cup honey

- 1/2 cup molasses

- 1 large egg

- 1 tablespoon lemon zest

- 1/4 cup finely chopped nuts (optional)

- 1/4 cup finely chopped dried fruit (optional)

- Instructions:

1. In a large bowl, whisk together the flour, baking powder, baking soda, spices, and salt.

2. In a separate bowl, cream together the sugar until light and fluffy.

3. Add the honey, molasses, egg, and lemon zest to the butter mixture and beat until well combined.

4. Gradually add the dry ingredients to the wet ingredients, mixing until a dough forms.

5. Stir in the chopped nuts and dried fruit, if using.

6. Wrap the dough in plastic wrap and refrigerate for at least 2 hours or overnight.

7. Preheat the oven to 350°F (175°C). Line baking sheets with parchment paper.

8. Roll out the dough on a lightly floured surface to about 1/4-inch thickness.

9. Cut out shapes using cookie cutters and place on the prepared baking sheets.

10. Bake for 10-12 minutes, or until the edges are lightly browned.

11. Allow the cookies to cool on the baking sheets for a few minutes before transferring to a wire rack to cool completely.

Christstollen Recipe:

- Ingredients:

  - 4 cups all-purpose flour

- 1/2 cup granulated sugar

- 1/2 teaspoon salt

- 1 package active dry yeast

- 3/4 cup warm milk

- 1/2 cup unsalted butter, softened

- 2 large eggs

- 1 teaspoon vanilla extract

- 1/2 teaspoon almond extract

- 1 cup mixed dried fruit (raisins, currants, candied orange peel)

- 1/2 cup chopped nuts (almonds, walnuts)

- 1/4 cup rum or brandy

- 1/2 cup marzipan (optional)

- Powdered sugar, for dusting

- Instructions:

1. In a large mixing bowl, combine the flour, sugar, salt, and yeast.

2. In a separate bowl, warm the milk and butter together until the butter is melted.

3. Add the milk mixture, eggs, vanilla, a
to the dry ingredients and mix until a dou

4. Knead the dough on a floured surface until smooth and elastic, about 10 minutes.

5. Place the dough in a greased bowl, cover, and let rise in a warm place for about 1 hour, or until doubled in size.

6. In a small bowl, combine the dried fruit, nuts, and rum or brandy. Let soak while the dough rises.

7. Punch down the dough and knead in the soaked fruit and nuts.

8. If using marzipan, roll it into a log and place it in the center of the dough, folding the dough over to enclose it.

9. Shape the dough into a loaf and place on a parchment-lined baking sheet. Cover and let rise for another 30 minutes.

10. Preheat the oven to 350°F (175°C).

11. Bake the Stollen for 35-40 minutes, or until golden brown.

12. While still warm, brush the loaf with melted butter and dust generously with powdered sugar.

13. Allow the Stollen to cool completely before slicing and serving.

WHERE TO FIND THE BEST FOOD STALLS IN EACH MARKET

Navigating the food stalls at a German Christmas market can be an adventure in itself. With so many delicious options, it can be difficult to know where to start. Here are some tips and recommendations for finding the best food stalls in a few of Germany's most famous Christmas markets.

1. Nuremberg Christkindlesmarkt: Nuremberg's Christkindlesmarkt is one of the oldest and most famous Christmas markets in Germany. It's also known for its outstanding food offerings, particularly its Nürnberger Rostbratwurst. Be sure to visit the Rauschgoldengel market stall, where you can try these delicious sausages grilled to perfection. For sweets, the Lebkuchen Schmidt stall is a must-visit, offering a wide variety of traditional gingerbread cookies.

2. Dresden Striezelmarkt: The Dresden Striezelmarkt is home to the world-famous Dresdner Christstollen. Look for the Stollenmeile, a row of stalls dedicated to this beloved holiday bread. Each stall offers its own version of Stollen,

so take the time to sample a few before deciding which one to take home. For a savory treat, head to the Kartoffelhaus stall, where you can enjoy crispy Kartoffelpuffer with a side of applesauce.

3. Cologne Christmas Market: Cologne's Christmas market is spread across several locations in the city, each with its own unique charm. The market at the Cologne Cathedral is a great place to find traditional German dishes like Reibekuchen (potato fritters) and Flammkuchen (a type of flatbread). For Glühwein, make your way to the Heinzelmännchen market in the Altstadt, where you'll find a wide variety of seasonal beverages, including hot chocolate with a shot of rum.

4. Munich Christkindlmarkt: Munich's Christkindlmarkt is known for its festive atmosphere and wide range of food options. Be sure to try the Weisswurst, a traditional Bavarian sausage served with sweet mustard and a pretzel. The market also has several stalls offering roasted chestnuts and candied nuts, perfect for snacking as you explore. For a sweet treat, visit the Elisenlebkuchen stall,

where you can sample some of the best gingerbread in the city.

5. Rothenburg ob der Tauber Reiterlesmarkt: Rothenburg's Reiterlesmarkt is a charming, small-town market that offers a more intimate experience. The market is famous for its Schneeballen, a local pastry made from strips of dough rolled into a ball, fried, and dusted with powdered sugar. You'll find several stalls selling these delicious treats, along with mulled wine and roasted nuts. For a savory option, try the bratwurst from the Bratwursthäusle stall, known for its smoky flavor and perfectly grilled sausages.

Tips for Navigating Food Options:
- Follow the Locals: If you see a long line of locals at a particular stall, it's usually a good sign that the food is worth the wait. Don't be afraid to ask for recommendations or strike up a conversation with other market-goers.
- Try Something New: While it's tempting to stick to familiar dishes, part of the fun of visiting a Christmas market is trying new foods. Look for regional specialties or seasonal dishes that you might not find elsewhere.

- Share and Sample: If you're traveling with friends or family, consider sharing dishes so that you can sample a wider variety of foods. Many stalls offer small portions or sampler platters, making it easy to try a little bit of everything.

- Bring Cash: While some stalls may accept credit cards, many operate on a cash-only basis. Be sure to bring enough euros with you to cover your food and drink purchases.

With these tips in hand, you'll be well-equipped to navigate the culinary delights of Germany's Christmas markets. Whether you're savoring a warm mug of Glühwein, biting into a crispy bratwurst, or indulging in a sweet piece of Stollen, the food and drink offerings at these markets are sure to be a highlight of your holiday season.

UNIQUE CHRISTMAS MARKET EXPERIENCES

German Christmas markets are more than just places to shop for holiday treats and gifts—they are full of unique experiences that create unforgettable memories. This chapter will take you on a journey through the many ways you can immerse yourself in the festive atmosphere.

From ice skating under twinkling lights to discovering one-of-a-kind artisan crafts, enjoying spectacular light shows, and finding activities that the entire family will love, these markets offer something special for everyone.

ICE SKATING AND WINTER SPORTS AT THE MARKETS

Winter sports are an integral part of the Christmas market experience in Germany. The magic of gliding on ice surrounded by festive decorations and the joyful sounds of holiday music is something that many visitors cherish.

Ice Skating:

One of the most popular winter activities at German Christmas markets is ice skating. Many markets, especially those in larger cities, feature beautifully decorated ice rinks right in the heart of the festivities. Imagine skating hand-in-hand with loved ones, the air crisp and cool, while fairy lights twinkle overhead. In markets like those in Berlin, Munich, and Cologne, the rinks are spacious and often surrounded by stalls offering warm drinks like Glühwein (mulled wine) and hot chocolate.

For beginners, many of these rinks offer skate rentals and even skating aids for children, so the whole family can join in the fun. In some locations, such as the market in Stuttgart, the ice rink is surrounded by grandstands where spectators can watch ice skating shows featuring talented local skaters, adding an extra layer of excitement to the experience.

Sledding:

While ice skating is widely available, some markets also offer sledding opportunities, particularly in regions with reliable snowfall. For example, the Christmas market in Garmisch-Partenkirchen, nestled in the Bavarian Alps, offers sledding hills that are perfect for families. The joy of racing down a hill on a wooden sled, the cold air rushing past, is a quintessential winter experience. These markets often have sleds available for rent, making it easy for visitors to join in on the fun.

Curling:

In some German Christmas markets, you can also try your hand at curling, a sport that combines skill, strategy, and a bit of luck. While it may not be as fast-paced as ice skating or sledding, curling is a social activity that's perfect for groups. Many markets set up small curling rinks where visitors can play a few rounds, often accompanied by friendly competition and laughter. This is especially popular in markets in the northern regions of Germany, where curling is a beloved winter pastime.

Winter Sports Beyond the Markets:

For those looking for even more winter sports, many Christmas markets are located near ski resorts or outdoor activity centers where visitors can enjoy a full day of skiing, snowboarding, or snowshoeing before heading to the market to warm up with a hot drink. The markets in towns like Oberstdorf and Berchtesgaden, for example, are surrounded by the stunning Bavarian Alps, offering visitors the perfect blend of outdoor adventure and holiday cheer.

ARTISAN CRAFTS AND HANDMADE GIFTS

One of the most charming aspects of German Christmas markets is the wide array of artisan crafts and handmade gifts. These items, often crafted by local artisans, make for truly unique holiday gifts that carry the spirit of German craftsmanship.

Traditional Christmas Ornaments:

At almost every market, you'll find stalls brimming with traditional German Christmas ornaments. These include hand-blown glass baubles, intricately carved wooden figures, and delicate straw stars. Markets in regions like the Erzgebirge (Ore Mountains) are especially famous for their wooden crafts, including the iconic nutcrackers and Christmas pyramids. Each piece is often made by hand using techniques passed down through generations, making them treasured keepsakes.

Handmade Textiles:

Another popular item at the markets is handmade textiles. From warm woolen scarves and hats to beautifully embroidered tablecloths and linens, these textiles showcase the skill of local weavers and embroiderers. In markets like those in Nuremberg and Dresden, you can find stalls dedicated to traditional Bavarian and Saxon clothing, including dirndls and lederhosen, all made with exquisite attention to detail.

Ceramics and Pottery:

Germany has a long history of pottery, and this is reflected in the many ceramics you'll find at Christmas markets. Hand-painted mugs, plates, and bowls in festive patterns make for wonderful gifts. Markets in regions like Thuringia and Bavaria are particularly known for their ceramics. These items often feature traditional motifs such as stars, angels, and winter scenes, making them perfect for holiday use or as decorative pieces.

Jewelry and Accessories:

Artisan jewelry is another highlight of the Christmas markets. From silver and amber necklaces to hand-beaded bracelets and earrings, there's something for every taste. Markets in cities like Hamburg and Frankfurt often feature stalls where local jewelers display their creations. Many of these pieces are one-of-a-kind, ensuring that your purchase is as unique as it is beautiful.

Toys and Games:

For those shopping for children, the markets offer a delightful array of handmade toys and games. Wooden toys, in particular, are a specialty, with items ranging from simple puzzles to intricately crafted dollhouses. In places like the Nuremberg Christmas market, you'll find entire stalls dedicated to traditional German toys, many of which are designed to be passed down through generations.

Where to Find the Best Artisan Crafts:

While almost every Christmas market will feature artisan crafts, some markets are particularly known for their high-quality handmade goods. The Nuremberg Christkindlesmarkt, for example, is famous for its traditional toys and Christmas decorations. The market in Rothenburg ob der Tauber is another must-visit, known for its handcrafted ornaments and textiles. For those seeking unique jewelry and accessories, the markets in Hamburg and Lübeck offer a fantastic selection.

LIGHT SHOWS AND HOLIDAY PERFORMANCES

The visual and auditory experiences at German Christmas markets are as much a part of the tradition as the shopping and eating. Spectacular light shows and festive holiday performances set the stage for a magical evening, creating memories that last long after the season has ended.

Light Shows:
As night falls, many Christmas markets come alive with dazzling light shows. These displays often use the architecture of the surrounding buildings as a canvas, projecting images of snowflakes, stars, and festive scenes in a mesmerizing array of colors. The Christmas market in Dresden, known as the Striezelmarkt, is famous for its light show, where the historic buildings of the Altmarkt are illuminated in a breathtaking spectacle.

In Berlin, the market at Gendarmenmarkt features one of the most elaborate light shows in the country. Here, the Französischer Dom and Deutscher Dom are bathed in a kaleidoscope of colors, while the central square is lit by hundreds of sparkling lights. The atmosphere is nothing short of magical, and it's easy to see why this market is a favorite among both locals and tourists.

Holiday Performances:

Live performances are another key feature of the Christmas markets, ranging from traditional carol singers to full-scale theatrical productions. In Cologne, the market at the Cathedral often hosts choral performances that echo through the square, creating a serene and spiritual atmosphere. These performances often include traditional German Christmas carols, many of which have been sung for centuries.

In Munich, the Christmas market at Marienplatz features daily performances by local musicians, playing everything from classical holiday music to contemporary festive songs. The market also hosts a "Krampus Run," where actors dressed as the fearsome Krampus—St. Nicholas's devilish companion—parade through the market, adding a bit of thrilling folklore to the festivities.

For those seeking more theatrical entertainment, some markets offer performances of classic holiday tales. The market in Stuttgart, for example, often includes live renditions of "The Nutcracker" or "A Christmas Carol," performed by local theater troupes. These performances are typically held in the evenings and are suitable for all ages, making them a perfect way to end a day at the market.

Tips for Experiencing Light Shows and Performances:
To fully enjoy the light shows and performances, it's a good idea to plan your visit around the scheduled events. Most markets will post a schedule of performances, so you can time your visit to catch a choral concert or light show. Arriving early is recommended, especially for popular performances, as seating or standing room can fill up quickly. For the best view of light shows, find a spot near the center of the square or along the edges of the market, where you can see the full display.

German Christmas markets are designed to be enjoyed by visitors of all ages, and there are plenty of activities that are perfect for families. From whimsical rides to hands-on workshops, these markets provide endless opportunities for children and adults alike to revel in the holiday spirit.

Children's Rides and Carousels:

Many Christmas markets feature traditional carousels, often beautifully decorated with hand-painted horses and carriages. These rides are a favorite among younger visitors and add a touch of nostalgia to the market experience. In larger markets like those in Hamburg and Leipzig, you'll also find more elaborate rides, such as Ferris wheels and mini-trains, which offer a bird's-eye view of the market below.

Petting Zoos and Nativity Scenes:

Another popular attraction for families is the inclusion of live nativity scenes and petting zoos. The market in Aachen, for example, features a charming nativity scene with real animals, allowing children to get up close to donkeys, sheep, and goats. This interactive element brings the Christmas story to life and is always a hit with younger visitors.

Storytelling and Puppet Shows:

In addition to rides and animals, many markets offer storytelling sessions and puppet shows, often based on traditional German fairy tales or holiday stories. These performances are usually held in cozy tents or small theaters within the market, creating an intimate setting where children can become engrossed in the tales of yesteryear. Markets like those in Freiburg and Heidelberg are particularly known for their excellent children's programs.

Craft Workshops:

For families looking to get hands-on, many markets offer craft workshops where children can create their own holiday decorations or gifts. These workshops might include activities like candle-making, ornament painting, or even gingerbread decorating. The market in Nuremberg is especially famous for its children's market, where kids can try their hand at a variety of crafts, guided by friendly artisans.

Family-Friendly Dining Options:

Of course, no trip to a Christmas market would be complete without sampling the delicious food, and many markets offer family-friendly dining options. Stalls selling bratwurst, pretzels, and roasted chestnuts are ubiquitous, but you'll also find stands offering sweet treats like waffles, crepes, and sugar-dusted pastries. For families with dietary restrictions, larger markets often have stalls offering vegetarian, vegan, and gluten-free options as well.

Tips for Enjoying the Markets with Children:

To ensure a fun and stress-free visit with children, it's best to go to the markets during the day or early evening when they are less crowded. Be sure to dress warmly, as the weather can be quite chilly, and consider bringing a stroller or baby carrier for younger children. Many markets also have designated family areas, with seating and facilities where you can take a break and warm up.

However, German Christmas markets are a treasure trove of experiences that cater to all ages and interests. Whether you're lacing up your skates for a spin on the ice, discovering the perfect handmade gift, marveling at a spectacular light show, or enjoying a carousel ride with your children, these markets offer a unique and unforgettable way to celebrate the holiday season. So bundle up, grab a warm drink, and let yourself be enchanted by the magic of a German Christmas market.

PLANNING YOUR CHRISTMAS MARKET TRIP

Planning a trip to Germany's Christmas markets is an exciting endeavor, but it's one that requires thoughtful consideration of dates, logistics, and accommodations. In this chapter, I'll guide you through the essential steps to make your visit as enjoyable and stress-free as possible, from selecting the best time to visit to navigating the bustling markets and finding the perfect place to stay. Let's dive in!

BEST TIMES TO VISIT: KEY DATES AND EVENTS

Germany's Christmas markets typically begin in late November and run through Christmas Eve, with some markets continuing until New Year's Eve or even into early January. While each market has its own schedule, here's a general timeline to help you plan your visit:

1. Late November (Week 4): Most of Germany's Christmas markets open during the last week of November. This is a wonderful time to visit if you want to experience the markets in their early stages, with fewer crowds and a more relaxed atmosphere. Key markets, such as those in Munich, Cologne, and Nuremberg, usually open during this week.

2. First Two Weeks of December: These weeks are considered prime time for visiting the markets. The festive spirit is in full swing, and the markets are bustling with activity. Special events such as St. Nicholas Day (December 6) add an extra layer of magic, especially in cities like Munich, where parades and processions are held.

3. Mid-December to Christmas Eve: As Christmas approaches, the markets become busier, especially on weekends. If you enjoy the lively hustle and bustle, this is the perfect time to soak in the festive atmosphere. However, it's important to be prepared for larger crowds, particularly at popular markets like those in Frankfurt and Berlin.

4. After Christmas (December 26 - January 1): Some markets remain open after Christmas, offering a quieter experience with post-holiday sales on handmade crafts and seasonal items. Cities like Berlin and Stuttgart often keep their markets open until the end of December or even into the first week of January, making this a great time for a more leisurely visit.

5. Special Events: Keep an eye out for unique events like Christmas concerts, ice-skating rinks, and themed nights. For example, the Dresden Striezelmarkt is famous for its Stollenfest, where a giant stollen cake is paraded through

the market, and the Heidelberg Christmas Market offers a beautiful ice rink set against the backdrop of the historic castle.

Pro Tip: Check each market's official website for the most up-to-date information on opening dates and special events, as these can vary slightly from year to year.

NAVIGATING THE MARKETS: TIPS FOR CROWDS AND WEATHER

Germany's Christmas markets are known for their festive charm, but they can also be crowded and chilly, especially during peak times. Here are some tips to help you navigate the markets with ease:

1. Timing Your Visit:

  - Weekdays vs. Weekends: Weekdays, particularly in the early afternoon, tend to be less crowded than weekends. If you can, plan your visit for a weekday to enjoy a more relaxed experience.

- Early Morning or Late Evening: Arriving early in the morning or later in the evening (after 7 PM) can help you avoid the peak crowds. The markets are particularly enchanting in the evening when the lights are twinkling, and the air is filled with the scent of mulled wine.

2. Weather Considerations:

- Dress in Layers: The weather can be quite cold, especially in the evenings, so dress in layers to stay warm. A good-quality winter coat, gloves, a hat, and a scarf are essential. Thermal undergarments can also make a big difference in keeping you comfortable.

- Footwear: Comfortable, warm, and waterproof footwear is a must, especially if you plan to walk a lot. Many markets are set up on cobblestone streets, so supportive shoes with good traction are recommended.

- Umbrellas and Rain Gear: While snow adds to the festive atmosphere, rain can be less pleasant. Carry a small, foldable umbrella and a waterproof jacket just in case.

3. Dealing with Crowds:

- Be Patient: Christmas markets are popular, and crowds are part of the experience. Stay patient and enjoy the festive atmosphere. If a particular stall is too crowded, move on and come back later.

- Pickpocket Awareness: Like any crowded place, it's important to be mindful of your belongings. Keep your valuables secure in a money belt or a crossbody bag that you can keep in front of you.

- Meeting Points: If you're traveling with others, agree on a meeting point in case you get separated in the crowd. The entrance or a well-known landmark within the market is a good choice.

4. Market Layouts:

- Grab a Map: Many markets provide maps at the entrance or on their websites. Familiarize yourself with the layout, including the locations of key attractions, food stalls, and restrooms.

- Rest and Warm-Up Spots: If you need a break, look for areas where you can sit and warm up. Many markets have heated tents or cafes nearby where you can enjoy a hot drink and relax for a bit.

5. Practical Tips:

- Cash is King: While more and more stalls accept cards, it's still a good idea to carry cash, especially in smaller towns or at traditional markets. ATMs are usually available nearby, but they can be busy.

- Reusable Cup Deposit: Many markets have a deposit system for their mulled wine mugs. You pay a small deposit, which you get back when you return the mug. However, many people choose to keep the mugs as souvenirs, so don't be surprised if you find yourself doing the same!

Pro Tip: If you're planning to visit multiple markets in one day, prioritize the ones that are less crowded or open earlier, and save the busier, more famous markets for the evening when they're fully lit up.

TRANSPORTATION: GETTING AROUND GERMANY DURING THE HOLIDAYS

Germany's extensive transportation network makes it easy to travel between cities and towns, even during the busy holiday season. Here's how to navigate your way around:

1. Public Transportation:

   - Trains: Germany's Deutsche Bahn (DB) is renowned for its efficiency and comfort. High-speed ICE trains connect major cities like Berlin, Munich, and Frankfurt, while regional trains (RE) and S-Bahn services are perfect for shorter journeys. During the holidays, trains can be busy, so it's advisable to book your tickets in advance, especially for long-distance travel.

- Christmas Market Trains: Some regions, such as Bavaria, offer special Christmas market train tickets that include discounts or group rates for visiting multiple markets. Check the DB website for seasonal offers and timetables.

- Public Transport in Cities: Most cities have excellent public transport systems, including buses, trams, and U-Bahn (subway) networks. Consider purchasing a day pass or a multi-day pass if you plan to explore a city extensively.

2. Car Rentals:

- Renting a Car: While trains are convenient, renting a car offers flexibility, especially if you're planning to visit smaller towns or remote markets. Major rental companies like Sixt, Europcar, and Hertz operate across Germany. Be sure to book in advance during the holiday season, and remember that winter tires are mandatory.

- Driving Tips: Germany's roads are well-maintained, but winter conditions can be challenging. Ensure your car is equipped with winter tires, and consider renting a car with four-wheel drive if you plan to visit mountainous regions. Parking can be difficult in city centers, so look for Park & Ride options where you can leave your car and take public transport into the city.

3. Local Travel Tips:

- Taxis and Rideshares: Taxis are widely available in cities, and rideshare services like Uber operate in major urban areas. However, taxis can be expensive, especially for longer distances.

- Walking and Biking: Many Christmas markets are located in pedestrian zones, making walking the best way to explore. Some cities, like Berlin, also have bike-sharing programs, but be cautious of icy conditions.

- Holiday Schedules: Be aware that public transportation operates on reduced schedules on public holidays, such as Christmas Eve and Christmas Day. Check timetables in advance to avoid any surprises.

Pro Tip: If you're planning to visit multiple cities, consider purchasing a German Rail Pass, which offers unlimited travel on the DB network for a set number of days. This can be a cost-effective option, especially if you plan to cover a lot of ground.

WHERE TO STAY: HOTELS AND ACCOMMODATIONS NEAR THE MARKETS

Finding the right accommodation can make or break your Christmas market experience. Here are some recommendations for hotels and lodgings near Germany's most popular markets:

1. Munich:

- Hotel Vier Jahreszeiten Kempinski Munich: Located in the heart of the city, this luxury hotel is within walking distance of the famous Marienplatz market. The elegant rooms and impeccable service make it a great choice for a special holiday stay.

- Contact Info: Maximilianstraße 17, 80539 Munich, Germany. Phone: +49 89 212520.

- Hotel Torbräu: A charming boutique hotel with a history dating back to 1490, Hotel Torbräu offers cozy accommodations and easy access to Munich's main Christmas markets.

- Contact Info: Tal 41, 80331 Munich, Germany. Phone: +49 89 242340.

2. Cologne:

- Excelsior Hotel Ernst: Just steps from the Cologne Cathedral and its renowned

Christmas market, this historic hotel offers luxurious rooms and an excellent dining experience. The festive decorations and proximity to the market make it a top choice.

- Contact Info: Trankgasse 1-5, 50667 Cologne, Germany. Phone: +49 221 2701.

- Hotel Lyskirchen: A stylish, modern hotel located near the Rhine, Hotel Lyskirchen is within walking distance of several of Cologne's Christmas markets. It's an excellent option for travelers seeking a balance of comfort and convenience.

- Contact Info: Filzengraben 26-32, 50676 Cologne, Germany. Phone: +49 221 9215930.

3. Nuremberg:

- Hotel Victoria: Situated at the entrance to the old town, this charming hotel is just a short walk from the famous Christkindlesmarkt. The Hotel Victoria offers a warm, welcoming atmosphere with beautifully appointed rooms.

- Contact Info: Königstraße 80, 90402 Nuremberg, Germany. Phone: +49 911 24050.

- NH Collection Nürnberg City: A modern hotel located close to the main train station and the historic city center, the NH Collection Nürnberg City offers spacious rooms and a relaxing spa, perfect for unwinding after a day at the market.

- Contact Info: Bahnhofstraße 17-19, 90402 Nuremberg, Germany. Phone: +49 911 99990.

4. Berlin:

- Hotel Adlon Kempinski: This iconic luxury hotel is located near Brandenburg Gate and is a short walk from several of Berlin's Christmas markets. The Hotel Adlon Kempinski is known for its opulent rooms, exceptional service, and festive atmosphere.

- Contact Info: Unter den Linden 77, 10117 Berlin, Germany. Phone: +49 30 22610.

- Hotel AMANO Grand Central: A modern hotel offering stylish accommodations, Hotel AMANO Grand Central is conveniently located near Berlin's main train station and several key Christmas markets.

- Contact Info: Heidestraße 62, 10557 Berlin, Germany. Phone: +49 30 4003000.

5. Stuttgart:

- Althoff Hotel am Schlossgarten: Overlooking the beautiful Schlossgarten park, this luxurious hotel is within walking distance of Stuttgart's Christmas market. The Althoff Hotel offers elegant rooms and a gourmet restaurant, making it a top choice for a festive stay.

- Contact Info: Schillerstraße 23, 70173 Stuttgart, Germany. Phone: +49 711 20260.

- Motel One Stuttgart-Hauptbahnhof: A budget-friendly option located near Stuttgart's main train station, Motel One offers modern, comfortable rooms and easy access to the city's Christmas market.

- Contact Info: Lautenschlagerstraße 14, 70173 Stuttgart, Germany. Phone: +49 711 3002090.

6. Dresden:

- Hotel Taschenbergpalais Kempinski: A luxurious hotel set in a historic palace, Hotel Taschenbergpalais Kempinski is just a short walk from Dresden's famous

Striezelmarkt. The grand architecture and opulent rooms make it a truly special place to stay.

- Contact Info: Taschenberg 3, 01067 Dresden, Germany. Phone: +49 351 49120.

- The Westin Bellevue Dresden: Located on the banks of the Elbe River, this hotel offers stunning views of the old town and is within easy reach of Dresden's Christmas markets. The Westin Bellevue combines modern comforts with classic elegance.

- Contact Info: Große Meißner Str. 15, 01097 Dresden, Germany. Phone: +49 351 8050.

Pro Tip: Book your accommodation as early as possible, especially if you're planning to visit during the peak holiday season. Many hotels offer special Christmas packages that include perks like mulled wine receptions or guided market tours.

With careful planning and the right resources, your Christmas market trip to Germany can be an unforgettable experience filled with joy, wonder, and a deep connection to the rich traditions of the holiday season. Whether you're navigating the bustling markets, sipping hot mulled wine, or relaxing in a cozy hotel after a day of exploration, this chapter has provided you with all the essential information to ensure your trip is as magical as the markets themselves. Enjoy every moment of your festive adventure!

LOCAL TRADITIONS AND CUSTOMS

THE ROLE OF THE CHRISTKIND AND OTHER HOLIDAY FIGURES

In Germany, Christmas is a time steeped in tradition, and no figure is as central to these celebrations as the Christkind, or "Christ Child." Unlike Santa Claus, who dominates the holiday imagery in many countries, the

Christkind is a figure rooted deeply in German culture, particularly in the southern regions like Bavaria and the Rhineland. The Christkind is traditionally depicted as a young, angelic figure, often with golden curls and dressed in a white robe, symbolizing purity and the spirit of Christmas. In some traditions, the Christkind is believed to be a manifestation of Jesus as a child, bringing gifts to children on Christmas Eve.

The origins of the Christkind can be traced back to the Protestant Reformation, when Martin Luther sought to shift the focus of Christmas away from Saint Nicholas, who had become associated with Catholicism. Luther introduced the Christkind as a way to emphasize the religious aspects of the holiday, particularly the birth of Christ. Today, the Christkind plays a central role in many German Christmas markets, where a young girl is often chosen to represent the figure, opening the markets with a speech and participating in various festive activities.

In addition to the Christkind, several other holiday figures play important roles in German Christmas traditions. One of these is Saint Nicholas, or Sankt Nikolaus, who is celebrated on December 6th. Saint Nicholas is a beloved figure who is known for his generosity and kindness, often bringing small gifts and treats to children who have been well-behaved. He is typically depicted as a bishop with a long white beard, wearing a red robe and carrying a staff. On the eve of Saint Nicholas Day, children leave out their shoes or boots in hopes that they will be filled with sweets and small gifts by the morning.

Another important figure is Knecht Ruprecht, who is often depicted as a darker, more menacing counterpart to Saint Nicholas. Knecht Ruprecht is said to accompany Saint Nicholas on his rounds, carrying a sack of coal or a bundle of switches to punish naughty children. Despite his fearsome appearance, Knecht Ruprecht serves as a reminder of the importance of good behavior and the consequences of misdeeds.

Finally, we have the Weihnachtsmann, or "Christmas Man," who is the German equivalent of Santa Claus. Unlike the Christkind, the Weihnachtsmann is a relatively modern figure, having gained popularity in Germany in the 19th century, influenced by the American version of Santa Claus. He is typically depicted as a jolly old man with a white beard, dressed in a red suit, and carrying a sack of gifts. The Weihnachtsmann is often seen as a more commercial figure, representing the modern aspects of Christmas celebrations.

These holiday figures, each with their unique roles and characteristics, contribute to the rich tapestry of German Christmas traditions, making the holiday season a magical and memorable time for all.

GERMAN CHRISTMAS CAROLS AND MUSIC AT THE MARKETS

Music is an integral part of the Christmas season in Germany, and no visit to a Christmas market would be complete without the sound of traditional German Christmas carols filling the air. These carols, known as "Weihnachtslieder," have been passed down through generations and are a cherished part of the holiday festivities. The melodies and lyrics evoke a sense of warmth, nostalgia, and the joyous spirit of the season.

One of the most famous German Christmas carols is "Stille Nacht, Heilige Nacht," known in English as "Silent Night." This beloved carol was composed in 1818 in the small Austrian town of Oberndorf, just across the border from Bavaria. The gentle, soothing melody and the message of peace and tranquility have made it a favorite around the world. The lyrics, originally written in German, speak of the serene and holy night when Christ was born:

"Stille Nacht, heilige Nacht,

Alles schläft, einsam wacht,

Nur das traute hochheilige Paar.

Holder Knabe im lockigen Haar,

Schlaf in himmlischer Ruh,

Schlaf in himmlischer Ruh."

Another popular carol that can be heard at German Christmas markets is "O Tannenbaum," a song that celebrates the Christmas tree, or "Tannenbaum." The carol originated in the 16th century and has become synonymous with the festive season. The lyrics, which praise the evergreen tree's resilience and beauty, are often sung as families gather around the Christmas tree to decorate it:

"O Tannenbaum, o Tannenbaum,

Wie treu sind deine Blätter!

Du grünst nicht nur zur Sommerzeit,

Nein, auch im Winter, wenn es schneit.

O Tannenbaum, o Tannenbaum,
Wie treu sind deine Blätter!"

In addition to these well-known carols, visitors to the markets will also hear traditional German folk songs, classical music, and performances by local choirs and brass bands. The sound of a choir singing "Es ist ein Ros entsprungen" (Lo, How a Rose E'er Blooming) or a brass band playing "Ihr Kinderlein, kommet" (O Come, Little Children) creates an atmosphere of joy and reverence, enhancing the magical experience of the markets.

Many Christmas markets also host live music performances, where local musicians and choirs perform both traditional and contemporary Christmas songs. These performances are often held in the evenings, as the markets are bathed in the soft glow of twinkling lights. The music, combined with the festive ambiance, makes for an unforgettable holiday experience.

CELEBRATING ADVENT: WREATHS, CALENDARS, AND RITUALS

Advent, the period leading up to Christmas, is a time of anticipation and preparation in Germany. It begins on the fourth Sunday before Christmas and is marked by various customs and traditions that bring a sense of joy and reflection to the season. The celebration of Advent is deeply rooted in German culture, with each week leading up to Christmas carrying its own significance and rituals.

One of the most iconic symbols of Advent in Germany is the Advent wreath, or "Adventskranz." The wreath is typically made of evergreen branches, symbolizing eternal life, and is adorned with four candles. Each Sunday during Advent, one candle is lit, accompanied by prayers or the singing of Christmas carols. The lighting of the candles is a moment of warmth and togetherness, as families gather around the wreath to reflect on the meaning of the season. The increasing light of the candles as Christmas approaches symbolizes the coming of Christ, the light of the world.

Another beloved tradition is the Advent calendar, or "Adventskalender." Originally created in Germany in the 19th century, the Advent calendar has become a popular tradition around the world. The calendar typically has 24 doors or windows, each of which is opened on the days leading up to Christmas, starting on December 1st. Behind each door, there is a small treat, such as a piece of chocolate, a toy, or a message of hope. The anticipation of opening each door adds to the excitement of the season, making the countdown to Christmas even more special, especially for children.

In addition to the wreath and calendar, there are various other rituals and customs associated with Advent in Germany. For example, many families participate in "Rorate" masses, early morning church services held during Advent. These masses are often celebrated by candlelight, creating a serene and contemplative atmosphere that allows worshippers to focus on the spiritual aspects of the season.

Baking is another cherished Advent tradition. German households are filled with the aroma of freshly baked "Plätzchen" (Christmas cookies) during this time. These cookies are often made using recipes that have been passed down through generations, and the baking process itself is a way for families to come together and share in the joy of the season. Popular types of cookies include "Lebkuchen" (gingerbread), "Zimtsterne" (cinnamon stars), and "Vanillekipferl" (vanilla crescent cookies).

The Advent season also sees the preparation of the "Weihnachtspyramide," a wooden Christmas pyramid that originated in the Erzgebirge (Ore Mountains) region of Germany. These pyramids are often decorated with nativity scenes and other Christmas figures, and they are powered by the heat of candles, which causes a carousel of figures to spin gently. The Weihnachtspyramide is a beautiful and intricate decoration that adds to the festive atmosphere of German homes and Christmas markets during Advent.

Overall, Advent in Germany is a time of joyous anticipation, filled with traditions that bring warmth and light to the dark days of winter. These customs help to create a sense of community and togetherness, as families and friends come together to celebrate the coming of Christmas.

HOLIDAY PARADES, EVENTS, AND FESTIVALS IN GERMAN CITIES

The Christmas season in Germany is marked by a vibrant array of parades, events, and festivals that take place in cities and towns across the country. These festive celebrations add an extra layer of excitement to the holiday season, drawing locals and visitors alike to partake in the joyful atmosphere.

One of the most famous holiday events is the Nuremberg Christkindlesmarkt, one of the oldest and most traditional Christmas markets in Germany. The market officially opens with the "Prologue," delivered by the Christkind herself from the balcony of the Frauenkirche (Church of Our Lady). The Christkind, played by a young woman chosen for her role, recites a poetic speech that has been handed down through generations, welcoming visitors to the market and setting the tone for the festivities. The opening ceremony is a grand event, drawing thousands of spectators and marking the beginning of the holiday season in Nuremberg.

In Munich, the Tollwood Winter Festival offers a unique blend of holiday cheer and cultural experiences. Held on the Theresienwiese, the same grounds as Oktoberfest, the Tollwood Festival features an eclectic mix of live music, theater performances, and artisan crafts. The festival is known for its alternative and eco-friendly approach, with a focus on sustainable practices and global cultural exchange. Visitors can enjoy a diverse range of food and drink options, from traditional German fare to international delicacies, while exploring the market's many stalls and entertainment offerings.

In Cologne, the city's Christmas markets are renowned for their stunning settings and festive atmosphere. The Cologne Cathedral Christmas Market, located in the shadow of the iconic Gothic cathedral, is a highlight of the season. Visitors can marvel at the impressive architecture while strolling through the market's charming stalls, which offer a wide array of handmade crafts, seasonal treats, and mulled wine. Another notable market in Cologne is the Rudolfplatz Christmas Market, known for its medieval theme and vibrant atmosphere, featuring a historical carousel and a range of artisanal products.

The city of Dresden hosts the Striezelmarkt, one of the largest and most historic Christmas markets in Germany. The market is named after the traditional Dresden Christmas Stollen, a rich fruit bread that is a specialty of the region. The Striezelmarkt offers visitors the chance to sample this festive treat, along with other local specialties, while enjoying live music, theatrical performances, and a large Christmas pyramid.

In Berlin, the capital city comes alive with numerous Christmas markets scattered throughout its neighborhoods. The Gendarmenmarkt Christmas Market, located in one of Berlin's most picturesque squares, features a stunning backdrop of historic buildings and offers a wide range of high-quality crafts, gourmet food, and entertainment. Another popular market is the Winterwald Market in the Prenzlauer Berg district, known for its cozy, rustic ambiance and focus on handmade goods.

In addition to the individual Christmas markets, many German cities also host festive parades and events throughout the holiday season. For example, the Christmas parade in Heidelberg is a beloved tradition that features colorful floats, live music, and performances by local choirs and bands. Similarly, the Christmas lights switch-on ceremony in Hamburg is a spectacular event that marks the beginning of the holiday season, with thousands of lights illuminating the city's streets and squares.

Throughout Germany, holiday festivals and events provide opportunities for communities to come together and celebrate the season with joy and enthusiasm. From the grandeur of the Nuremberg Christkindlesmarkt to the charming local markets in smaller towns, these celebrations capture the essence of German Christmas traditions and offer a memorable experience for visitors and locals alike.

In summary, German Christmas markets and traditions are rich with history and cultural significance. The Christkind and other holiday figures bring a sense of magic and wonder to the season, while the music, Advent customs, and festive events create an atmosphere of warmth and joy. Whether you're exploring the bustling markets of Munich, enjoying the historical charm of Nuremberg, or experiencing the vibrant celebrations of Berlin, the holiday season in Germany offers a unique and unforgettable experience that embodies the true spirit of Christmas.

BEYOND THE MARKETS: EXPLORING GERMANY IN WINTER

The Bavarian Alps

Winter in Germany offers more than just enchanting Christmas markets. As the snow blankets the land and the days grow shorter, a different kind of magic unfolds across the country. From majestic winter landscapes that invite outdoor adventures to castles, museums, and historic sites that come alive during the holidays, Germany provides a wealth of experiences that go beyond the twinkling lights and festive stalls. In this chapter, we will explore the best of Germany in winter, taking you on a journey through its breathtaking scenery and cultural treasures.

WINTER LANDSCAPES AND OUTDOOR ADVENTURES

Germany's winter landscapes are a symphony of snow-covered forests, frozen lakes, and mountain peaks piercing the frosty skies. Whether you are an adventurer seeking thrills or someone who prefers serene strolls through picturesque settings, Germany's diverse geography offers something for everyone during the colder months.

The Bavarian Alps: A Winter Wonderland

The Bavarian Alps are perhaps the most iconic winter destination in Germany. These snow-clad mountains, with their sharp peaks and deep valleys, offer endless opportunities for outdoor enthusiasts. Garmisch-Partenkirchen, a town nestled in the heart of the Alps, is a gateway to some of the best skiing in Germany. Here, the Zugspitze, Germany's highest peak, towers at 2,962 meters, providing a dramatic backdrop for winter sports. Skiers and snowboarders flock to the slopes, which cater to all levels of expertise, from beginner-friendly trails to more challenging descents.

But it's not just about skiing. The Bavarian Alps also offer activities such as snowshoeing and tobogganing. Snowshoeing through the quieter trails of the Alps allows you to experience the peacefulness of the snow-covered forests, where the only sound is the crunch of snow beneath your feet. For something more exhilarating, toboggan runs like the one on Mount Wallberg offer a thrilling ride down the mountain.

For those seeking a more relaxed experience, winter hiking is a popular activity in this region. The Alps are crisscrossed with well-marked trails that take you through fairy-tale forests, past frozen waterfalls, and to panoramic viewpoints where you can take in the majesty of the snow-covered landscape. One of the most picturesque routes is the Partnach Gorge, where the river's icy sculptures create a mesmerizing natural gallery.

The Black Forest: A Snow-Draped Fairytale

The Black Forest, with its dense woodlands and charming villages, transforms into a magical winter wonderland when covered in snow. Located in southwestern Germany, this region is famous for its dark, towering trees and half-timbered houses that look even more enchanting with a layer of fresh snow.

Titisee Lake, one of the most popular destinations in the Black Forest, freezes over in winter, offering a perfect setting for ice skating. Surrounded by snowy hills and dense forest, gliding over the frozen lake feels like stepping into a winter postcard. If you're looking for more adventure, nearby Feldberg Mountain, the highest peak in the Black Forest, offers excellent skiing and snowboarding options. Feldberg is also a fantastic spot for winter hiking, with trails leading through snow-covered landscapes to viewpoints that offer stunning vistas over the entire region.

For a more peaceful winter experience, the Black Forest also offers several thermal baths and spas, where you can relax and rejuvenate after a day in the snow. Baden-Baden, a historic spa town on the edge of the Black Forest, is renowned for its thermal baths, including the elegant Friedrichsbad, where you can soak in warm mineral waters while admiring the beautiful 19th-century architecture.

The Harz Mountains: A Winter Adventure Playground

The Harz Mountains, located in central Germany, are a hidden gem for winter sports enthusiasts. Known for their rugged beauty and rich folklore, the Harz Mountains offer a variety of outdoor activities, from skiing and snowboarding to snowshoeing and sledding.

The town of Braunlage is the heart of winter sports in the Harz region. The Wurmberg ski area offers a range of slopes for skiing and snowboarding, as well as Germany's longest toboggan run, which stretches over 1,500 meters. For those who prefer cross-country skiing, the Harz Mountains are crisscrossed with hundreds of kilometers of well-maintained trails, leading through dense forests and across open plateaus.

One of the most unique winter experiences in the Harz Mountains is the Brockenbahn, a historic steam train that takes you to the summit of the Brocken, the highest peak in the region. As the train chugs up the mountain, it passes through snow-covered forests and offers breathtaking views over the surrounding landscape. At the summit, you can explore the mystical Brocken plateau, which is often shrouded in mist and has inspired many local legends.

For a more tranquil experience, winter hiking in the Harz Mountains is a great way to explore the region's natural beauty. Trails like the Hexenstieg (Witches' Trail) take you through ancient forests, past frozen waterfalls, and to scenic viewpoints where you can take in the rugged winter landscape.

Saxon Switzerland: Winter Hiking and Rock Climbing

Saxon Switzerland, a national park located in eastern Germany near the Czech border, is a paradise for outdoor enthusiasts, even in winter. Known for its dramatic sandstone formations and deep gorges, this region offers some of the most unique winter landscapes in Germany.

Winter hiking in Saxon Switzerland is a magical experience. The snow-covered sandstone cliffs and frozen rivers create a stunning contrast against the blue winter sky. One of the most popular winter hiking trails is the Malerweg (Painter's Way), a route that takes you through the most scenic parts of the national park, including the famous Bastei Bridge, which offers breathtaking views over the Elbe River and the surrounding cliffs.

For the more adventurous, Saxon Switzerland also offers winter rock climbing. While many of the more challenging routes are off-limits during the winter months, there are still plenty of opportunities for experienced climbers to tackle the sandstone cliffs. The region's unique rock formations make for an exhilarating climbing experience, with the added challenge of snow and ice.

After a day of exploring, you can warm up in one of the region's cozy guesthouses or enjoy a traditional meal at a local inn. Saxon Switzerland is also home to several charming villages, such as Bad Schandau and Königstein, where you can experience the warmth and hospitality of the local people.

VISITING CASTLES, MUSEUMS, AND HISTORIC SITES DURING THE HOLIDAYS

Germany's rich history is woven into its castles, museums, and historic sites, many of which take on a special charm during the winter holiday season. From grand palaces adorned with festive decorations to museums offering special exhibitions, winter is a fantastic time to delve into the cultural heritage of Germany.

Neuschwanstein Castle: A Fairytale Winter Escape

Neuschwanstein Castle, nestled in the Bavarian Alps, is one of the most famous castles in the world, and it becomes even more enchanting during the winter months. With its turrets and towers dusted with snow, Neuschwanstein looks like something out of a fairytale. Built by King Ludwig II, the castle is a testament to the king's romantic imagination, and its interiors are filled with lavish decorations and stunning murals.

During the holiday season, Neuschwanstein takes on a special atmosphere, with fewer crowds and a serene winter landscape surrounding the castle. The nearby town of Füssen, with its charming streets and festive lights, is also worth exploring, and the surrounding area offers excellent opportunities for winter hiking and snowshoeing.

Another nearby castle, Hohenschwangau, which was Ludwig II's childhood home, is also open to visitors during the winter. The contrast between the two castles—Neuschwanstein's dreamlike grandeur and Hohenschwangau's more traditional charm—makes for a fascinating day of exploration.

Heidelberg Castle: Winter Magic in the Romantic City

Heidelberg is one of Germany's most romantic cities, and its castle, perched high above the old town, is a must-visit destination during the winter months. Heidelberg Castle, a mix of Gothic and Renaissance architecture, is especially magical in winter when it is often dusted with snow, and the views over the Neckar River and the old town below are breathtaking.

The castle's expansive grounds are open for winter walks, offering a peaceful escape from the hustle and bustle of the city. Inside, the Heidelberg Castle Museum provides a fascinating look into the history of the castle and the region. During the holiday season, the castle also hosts special events, including winter tours and Christmas concerts, adding to the festive atmosphere.

Heidelberg itself is a charming city to explore during the winter months. The old town is filled with cozy cafes and traditional German restaurants where you can warm up with a cup of Glühwein (mulled wine) or enjoy a hearty meal after a day of sightseeing.

Sanssouci Palace: A Royal Winter Retreat
Sanssouci Palace, located in Potsdam near Berlin, was the summer retreat of Frederick the Great, but it takes on a special charm during the winter months. The palace, with its beautiful Baroque architecture and stunning gardens, is a UNESCO World Heritage site and one of the most important cultural landmarks in Germany.

In winter, the gardens of Sanssouci are transformed into a peaceful winter wonderland, with snow-covered paths leading through the terraced vineyards and past the elegant fountains. The palace itself is open for tours, and its opulent interiors are a testament to the grandeur of the Prussian royal court. During the holiday season, Sanssouci offers special guided tours that focus on the winter traditions of the Prussian kings, providing a unique insight into royal life.

Potsdam, with its historic palaces and charming old town, is also worth exploring during the winter months. The city's Dutch Quarter, with its red-brick houses and cozy cafes, is particularly atmospheric in winter, and the nearby New Palace and Cecilienhof Palace are also open to visitors during the holiday season.

Nuremberg: History and Tradition

Nuremberg is known for its world-famous Christmas market, but the city's rich history makes it worth exploring beyond the market stalls. The Nuremberg Castle, perched on a hill overlooking the old town, is a symbol of the city's medieval past. During the winter months, the castle's stone walls and towers are often covered in snow, adding to the sense of history and tradition that permeates the city.

The castle complex includes the Imperial Castle Museum, which provides a fascinating look into the history of the Holy Roman Empire and the role Nuremberg played in medieval Germany. The views from the castle ramparts over the snow-covered rooftops of the old town are particularly stunning in winter.

Nuremberg is also home to several important museums, including the Germanic National Museum, which houses one of the largest collections of German art and culture in the world. During the holiday season, the museum offers special exhibitions and events, making it a great place to explore the cultural heritage of Germany during your winter visit.

Berlin: A City of Museums and History

Berlin is a city that is steeped in history, and its many museums and historic sites make it a must-visit destination during the winter months. The city's Museum Island, a UNESCO World Heritage site, is home to some of the most important museums in Germany, including the Pergamon Museum, the Altes Museum, and the Neues Museum. These museums offer a rich collection of art and artifacts, from ancient sculptures to 19th-century paintings, and are a perfect place to escape the winter cold and delve into the history of human civilization.

Berlin is also home to several important historic sites, including the Brandenburg Gate, the Berlin Wall Memorial, and the Reichstag. During the holiday season, many of these sites are illuminated with festive lights, adding to the city's vibrant atmosphere. The Berlin Cathedral, with its majestic dome, is particularly beautiful in winter, and the views from its observation deck over the snow-covered city are breathtaking.

In addition to its museums and historic sites, Berlin is also known for its winter festivals and events. The city's Christmas markets are some of the best in Germany, and during the holiday season, Berlin comes alive with festive lights, ice skating rinks, and holiday concerts.

DAY TRIPS AND EXCURSIONS FROM MAJOR MARKET CITIES

Germany's major market cities—such as Berlin, Munich, Frankfurt, and Cologne—are excellent hubs for exploring the surrounding regions. Winter provides a unique opportunity to experience the quieter side of German cities, as well as picturesque countryside, charming villages, and historic landmarks. Whether you're interested in natural wonders, history, or cultural experiences, these day trips are perfect for discovering Germany beyond the markets.

From Berlin: Potsdam and Sanssouci Palace

A short 45-minute train ride from Berlin, Potsdam is a UNESCO World Heritage city known for its magnificent palaces and gardens. Sanssouci Palace, often referred to as the "German Versailles," is a must-visit in winter when the palace's Baroque beauty is accentuated by the soft light of the season. The palace grounds are stunning, even in winter, with manicured gardens, ornamental fountains, and historic buildings. A stroll through Potsdam's Dutch Quarter and Old Market Square offers a glimpse into the city's rich history and picturesque architecture.

From Munich: Neuschwanstein Castle and the Bavarian Alps

No trip to Bavaria is complete without visiting the iconic Neuschwanstein Castle, a true fairy-tale structure nestled in the Bavarian Alps. A two-hour train ride from Munich, this stunning castle inspired Disney's Sleeping Beauty Castle and is even more magical in winter when it's surrounded by snow-covered mountains. The nearby town of Füssen is also worth exploring, with its charming old town, frozen lakes, and alpine scenery. For outdoor enthusiasts, winter hiking or sledding in the surrounding mountains is a perfect way to experience the beauty of Bavaria in winter.

From Frankfurt: Heidelberg and the Romantic Rhine Valley

Heidelberg, with its historic castle and picturesque old town, is a charming destination for a day trip from Frankfurt. Just an hour away by train, this university town is especially enchanting in winter, with its cobbled streets, traditional German architecture, and the Neckar River flowing through the city. A visit to Heidelberg Castle offers breathtaking views of the city and the surrounding valley. Another option is to explore the Romantic Rhine Valley, famous for its vineyards, medieval castles, and charming towns like Rüdesheim.

Winter boat cruises along the Rhine are a serene way to experience this UNESCO World Heritage site.

From Cologne: Aachen and Monschau

Aachen, located just an hour from Cologne by train, is famous for its stunning cathedral, which is a UNESCO World Heritage site and one of the oldest in Europe. The city's rich history and connection to Charlemagne make it a fascinating destination. Aachen is also known for its thermal baths, which are perfect for warming up on a chilly winter day. Another nearby gem is Monschau, a picturesque town in the Eifel region known for its half-timbered houses and scenic setting in a narrow valley. Monschau's Christmas market, though smaller than Cologne's, is charming and offers a more intimate holiday experience.

From Hamburg: Lübeck and the Baltic Sea

Lübeck, a UNESCO World Heritage city and the former capital of the Hanseatic League, is just an hour from

Hamburg and is renowned for its medieval architecture and marzipan. The city's Holstentor gate and old town are particularly beautiful in winter, with snow-dusted rooftops and festive decorations. Lübeck is also a gateway to the Baltic Sea, and a visit to the seaside town of Travemünde offers a refreshing contrast to the bustling markets of Hamburg. The Baltic coastline, with its long sandy beaches and rugged cliffs, is serene and beautiful in winter, making it an ideal destination for a peaceful day trip.

From Stuttgart: The Black Forest and Lake Constance

The Black Forest, with its dense forests, picturesque villages, and snow-covered hills, is one of Germany's most iconic regions. Just a short drive or train ride from Stuttgart, this region is perfect for a winter getaway. Visit the charming town of Triberg, home to Germany's highest waterfall and famous for its cuckoo clocks, or explore the scenic beauty of the Black Forest by taking a winter hike or sleigh ride through the snow-covered landscape. Another great option is a day trip to Lake Constance, where you can enjoy stunning views of the lake and the surrounding Alps, as well as visit the charming towns of Konstanz and Meersburg.

SEASONAL EVENTS: NEW YEAR'S EVE, EPIPHANY, AND BEYOND

Winter in Germany is not just about Christmas; the festive spirit continues into the New Year and beyond. From lively New Year's Eve celebrations to traditional Epiphany festivities, there are numerous events that keep the holiday spirit alive throughout the winter months. Here's a look at some of the most notable seasonal events in Germany and how to experience them.

New Year's Eve (Silvester)

New Year's Eve, known as Silvester in Germany, is celebrated with great enthusiasm across the country. Major cities like Berlin, Munich, and Frankfurt host spectacular fireworks displays, parties, and events that attract both locals and visitors.

- Berlin: The New Year's Eve celebration in Berlin is one of the largest in Europe, with over a million people gathering at the Brandenburg Gate for a massive open-air party. The highlight of the night is the fireworks display at midnight, which lights up the sky above Berlin's iconic landmarks. The celebrations continue into the early hours with live music, DJ sets, and street parties throughout the city. For those seeking a more traditional experience, many restaurants offer special New Year's Eve dinners, and river cruises on the Spree offer a unique perspective of the city's fireworks.

- Munich: Munich's New Year's Eve celebrations are centered around Marienplatz, the heart of the city. The lively atmosphere, combined with the beautiful backdrop of Munich's historic buildings, makes this a memorable place to ring in the New Year. Fireworks displays can be seen across the city, and many locals gather at public squares or in the Englischer Garten to watch the spectacle. After midnight, the city's bars, clubs, and beer halls are filled with revelers celebrating well into the night.

- Frankfurt: Frankfurt's skyline provides the perfect setting for a dazzling New Year's Eve fireworks display. The Main Riverbank is a popular spot for watching the fireworks, with the city's modern skyscrapers reflecting the bursts of color. The Sachsenhausen district is known for its lively pubs and clubs, where you can continue the celebrations after the fireworks.

Epiphany (Heilige Drei Könige)

Epiphany, or Heilige Drei Könige (Three Kings' Day), is celebrated on January 6th and marks the end of the Christmas season in Germany. This religious holiday commemorates the visit of the Three Wise Men to the baby Jesus and is an important day in many parts of the country, especially in the predominantly Catholic regions of Bavaria and Baden-Württemberg.

- Bavaria: In Bavaria, Epiphany is a public holiday, and many towns and villages hold special church services, processions, and reenactments of the Three Wise Men's journey. In some areas, children dressed as the Three Kings go from house to house, singing carols and blessing homes with chalk inscriptions on the doors. This tradition, known as Sternsingen, is a way of raising money for charity and is a cherished part of Bavarian culture.

- Baden-Württemberg: The Swabian region of Baden-Württemberg also celebrates Epiphany with various customs and traditions. In many towns, you'll find processions and parades, where participants dress in traditional costumes and reenact the biblical story. Epiphany concerts and performances are also common, with churches hosting special events to mark the occasion.

Fasching and Karneval

While Epiphany marks the end of the Christmas season, it also signals the beginning of the Fasching (or Karneval) season in Germany. This pre-Lenten celebration, which takes place in the weeks leading up to Ash Wednesday, is filled with parades, parties, and colorful costumes.

- Cologne: Cologne's Karneval is one of the most famous in Germany, and the city is transformed into a vibrant celebration of music, dancing, and fun. The highlight of the festivities is the Rose Monday Parade (Rosenmontagszug), which features elaborate floats, marching bands, and participants in wild costumes. Karneval is a time for letting loose, and the streets of Cologne are filled with revelers enjoying the festive atmosphere.

- Mainz: Mainz, another city with a strong Karneval tradition, hosts a series of events leading up to Rose Monday. The city's parade is known for its political satire, with floats poking fun at current events and politicians. The atmosphere in Mainz during Karneval is lively and fun, with everyone getting into the spirit of the season.

Winter Festivals and Markets

While most Christmas markets close after the holiday, some continue into January, and there are also a variety of winter festivals that keep the festive spirit alive.

- Stuttgart Winter Festival: Stuttgart's Winter Festival, held in the city's Palace Square, is a celebration of winter sports and activities. The festival features an ice rink, curling lanes, and winter-themed stalls offering food, drinks, and crafts. It's a great way to enjoy the winter season even after the Christmas markets have closed.

- Winter Tollwood Festival (Munich): Munich's Winter Tollwood Festival, held at the Theresienwiese (the same site as Oktoberfest), is a cultural event that combines art, music, and eco-consciousness. The festival features a wide range of performances, from live music and theater to acrobatics and dance, as well as an international market with food and crafts from around the world. The festival runs from late November to New Year's Eve, with a special New Year's Eve party that attracts thousands of visitors.

- Hamburg Winter Dom: The Hamburg Winter Dom is a large winter fair held on the city's Heiligengeistfeld. It's the largest funfair in Northern Germany and offers a variety of rides, games, and food stalls. The Winter Dom is a family-friendly event with something for everyone, from thrilling roller coasters to cozy mulled wine stands.

Winter Sports and Outdoor Activities

For those who love the outdoors, Germany's winter landscape offers plenty of opportunities for winter sports and activities. From skiing and snowboarding in the Alps to ice skating and sledding in city parks, there are countless ways to enjoy the winter season.

- Skiing in the Bavarian Alps: Germany's Bavarian Alps are a winter sports paradise, with ski resorts catering to all levels of skiers and snowboarders. Popular resorts include Garmisch-Partenkirchen, Oberstdorf, and Berchtesgaden, which offer well-groomed slopes, cozy alpine lodges, and stunning mountain views. For those new to skiing, many resorts offer lessons and beginner-friendly slopes.

- Ice Skating in Berlin: Berlin's winter parks and outdoor ice rinks are perfect for ice skating enthusiasts. The city's largest ice rink, the Horst-Dohm Ice Stadium, offers plenty of space for skaters of all levels. Other popular ice skating venues include the outdoor rink at Potsdamer Platz, which is surrounded by festive lights and holiday decorations, making it a magical place to skate.

- Sledding in the Black Forest: The Black Forest is not only a great destination for hiking and sightseeing but also for winter sports. Sledding is a popular activity in the region, with many hills and trails offering the perfect terrain for a thrilling ride. The Feldberg, the highest mountain in the Black Forest, is a popular spot for sledding, with well-maintained runs that are fun for all ages.

Germany in winter is a country of contrasts – from the lively, festive atmosphere of its Christmas markets to the serene beauty of its snow-covered landscapes. Beyond the markets, there's a wealth of experiences waiting to be discovered. Whether you're exploring fairy-tale castles, hiking through a snowy forest, or taking part in traditional holiday celebrations, winter in Germany offers a unique blend of adventure, culture, and charm.

APPENDICES

CHRISTMAS MARKET CALENDAR: DATES AND HIGHLIGHTS

The Christmas market season is one of the most magical times of the year in Germany. With snow-dusted streets, twinkling lights, and the aroma of mulled wine wafting through the air, German cities transform into festive wonderlands. To make the most of your trip, it's important to plan your visit around the opening dates and special events of each market. Below is a detailed Christmas Market Calendar for 2024-2025, highlighting the most popular markets in Germany along with key dates and festive events.

1. Munich Christkindlmarkt (Munich)
- Opening Date: November 27, 2024
- Closing Date: December 24, 2024
- Highlights: The grand opening ceremony at Marienplatz is a must-see, featuring the lighting of the Christmas tree and performances by local choirs. Don't

miss the Krampus Run (Krampuslauf), where costumed figures parade through the streets in a nod to Bavarian folklore.

2. Nuremberg Christkindlesmarkt (Nuremberg)
- Opening Date: November 29, 2024
- Closing Date: December 24, 2024
- Highlights: The Nuremberg Christkind opens the market with a traditional prologue, an event that attracts thousands of visitors. The market is also famous for its handcrafted ornaments and the delightful Zwetschgenmännle (plum people).

3. Cologne Christmas Markets (Cologne)
- Opening Date: November 25, 2024
- Closing Date: December 23, 2024
- Highlights: Cologne boasts several Christmas markets, but the most famous is the one at Cologne Cathedral. The backdrop of the towering Gothic cathedral makes for an unforgettable experience. Enjoy ice skating at the

Christmas market in the Old Town or take a ride on the historic carousel at the Harbour Christmas Market.

4. Dresden Striezelmarkt (Dresden)
- Opening Date: November 28, 2024
- Closing Date: December 24, 2024
- Highlights: As Germany's oldest Christmas market, the Striezelmarkt has a rich history dating back to 1434. The market is named after the Striezel, a traditional German cake that later evolved into the famous Dresden Stollen. Don't miss Stollenfest, where a giant Stollen cake is paraded through the streets.

5. Stuttgart Christmas Market (Stuttgart)
- Opening Date: November 27, 2024
- Closing Date: December 23, 2024
- Highlights: Stuttgart's Christmas Market is one of the largest in Germany, with over 280 beautifully decorated stalls. The Finnish Christmas Village within the market

offers a unique cultural experience with Nordic specialties like reindeer meat and glögi (mulled wine).

6. Frankfurt Christmas Market (Frankfurt)
- Opening Date: November 25, 2024
- Closing Date: December 22, 2024
- Highlights: Located in the Römerberg and St. Paul's Square, the Frankfurt Christmas Market is one of the oldest in Germany. Enjoy traditional apple wine and Bethmännchen (marzipan cookies), and experience the festive atmosphere with concerts, carols, and puppet shows.

7. Leipzig Christmas Market (Leipzig)
- Opening Date: November 26, 2024
- Closing Date: December 22, 2024
- Highlights: Leipzig's market dates back to 1458 and features over 250 stalls spread across the historic city center. Special events include the fairytale forest, the

traditional Christmas concert by the St. Thomas Boys Choir, and the medieval market at the Naschmarkt.

8. Rothenburg ob der Tauber Reiterlesmarkt (Rothenburg ob der Tauber)
- Opening Date: November 29, 2024
- Closing Date: December 23, 2024
- Highlights: The charming medieval town of Rothenburg ob der Tauber transforms into a Christmas fairytale during the Reiterlesmarkt. The market is named after the Reiterle, a mystical horseman from German folklore who once ushered in the winter season. The market offers a unique blend of tradition and fantasy.

9. Berlin Christmas Markets (Berlin)
- Opening Date: November 27, 2024
- Closing Date: December 31, 2024
- Highlights: Berlin hosts over 60 Christmas markets, each with its own character. The Gendarmenmarkt Christmas Market is a standout, known for its artisan

crafts and gourmet food. The Winter World at Potsdamer Platz offers ice skating, curling, and snow tubing for the more adventurous visitors.

10. Hamburg Christmas Markets (Hamburg)
- Opening Date: November 25, 2024
- Closing Date: December 23, 2024
- Highlights: The historic Christmas market in front of the Hamburg Town Hall is a highlight, with its mix of traditional and modern stalls. Don't miss the flying Santa, who soars above the market three times a day in a sleigh. The Fleetinsel Christmas Market offers a maritime twist with its harbor views and unique decorations.

11. Lübeck Christmas Market (Lübeck)
- Opening Date: November 27, 2024
- Closing Date: January 5, 2025
- Highlights: Lübeck's Christmas market extends into the new year, allowing visitors to enjoy the festive

atmosphere a bit longer. The UNESCO World Heritage site of Lübeck's Old Town is a beautiful backdrop for this market, which is famous for its marzipan and historical crafts.

12. Essen International Christmas Market (Essen)
- Opening Date: November 23, 2024
- Closing Date: December 23, 2024
- Highlights: With over 250 stalls representing 20 different nations, Essen's International Christmas Market is a multicultural celebration. Enjoy food and crafts from around the world, including Finnish candles, Russian nesting dolls, and French crêpes.

Special Events and Festivals

Christmas Eve Mass at Cologne Cathedral (Cologne)
- Date: December 24, 2024

- Description: Experience the spiritual side of Christmas by attending midnight mass at Cologne Cathedral, one of the most famous religious services in Germany.

St. Nicholas Day (Nationwide)
- Date: December 6, 2024
- Description: Celebrate St. Nicholas Day, when children leave their shoes out to be filled with sweets and gifts by St. Nicholas. Many markets host special events for this festive day.

Feuerzangenbowle Night (Various Locations)
- Date: Throughout December
- Description: Feuerzangenbowle is a traditional German holiday punch made by caramelizing sugar over mulled wine. Many markets host Feuerzangenbowle nights, where visitors can watch the preparation of this fiery drink and enjoy a warm glass in the chilly winter air.

ESSENTIAL PACKING LIST FOR YOUR CHRISTMAS MARKET TRIP

When visiting Germany's Christmas markets, it's important to be prepared for cold weather and festive activities. Packing appropriately will ensure you stay warm, comfortable, and ready to enjoy everything from mulled wine to ice skating. Below is a comprehensive packing list tailored to winter travel and Christmas market exploration.

Clothing

1. Warm Coat
- Description: A heavy, insulated coat is essential for staying warm in the cold German winter. Look for options that are water-resistant and windproof to handle all weather conditions.

2. Thermal Layers

- Description: Pack thermal tops and leggings to wear under your clothes. These will keep you warm without adding bulk, making it easier to move around and explore the markets.

3. Sweaters

- Description: Bring a few cozy sweaters for layering. Wool and cashmere are excellent options for warmth.

4. Scarf, Hat, and Gloves

- Description: A thick scarf, insulated gloves, and a woolen hat are must-haves to protect against the cold. Opt for touchscreen gloves so you can use your phone without exposing your hands to the elements.

5. Waterproof Boots

- Description: Comfortable, waterproof boots with good insulation and traction are vital for walking around icy and wet markets. Make sure they're broken in before your trip to avoid blisters.

6. Wool Socks

- Description: Pack multiple pairs of thick wool socks to keep your feet warm and dry. Wool is a great material for wicking moisture away while providing insulation.

7. Jeans or Warm Trousers

- Description: A pair of warm, comfortable trousers or jeans is ideal for casual market visits. Consider fleece-lined options for extra warmth.

8. Umbrella

- Description: A small, compact umbrella can come in handy during unexpected rain or snow showers.

Accessories

1. Crossbody Bag or Backpack

- Description: A secure, hands-free bag is ideal for carrying your essentials while navigating crowded markets. Choose one with multiple compartments to keep everything organized.

2. Reusable Shopping Bag
- Description: Bring along a reusable shopping bag for any purchases. Many markets sell unique, handcrafted items that you'll want to take home.

3. Refillable Water Bottle
- Description: While you'll likely be sipping on hot drinks, staying hydrated is still important. A refillable water bottle with a built-in filter can be handy.

4. Portable Phone Charger
- Description: Keep your phone charged for photos, maps, and translations by bringing a portable charger. Winter cold can drain battery life quickly.

Personal Care

1. Lip Balm
- Description: Cold weather can dry out your lips, so pack a good lip balm with SPF for protection.

2. Hand Cream
- Description: Keep your hands moisturized with a rich hand cream. Cold weather and frequent handwashing can cause dry skin.

3. Sunscreen
- Description: Even in winter, the sun's rays can be harsh, especially if you're outside all day. Apply a layer of sunscreen to exposed skin.

4. Travel Tissues
- Description: Pack travel-sized tissues for the inevitable cold weather sniffles. They're also useful for impromptu cleanups.

5. Hand Sanitizer

- Description: With so many people around, it's a good idea to keep hand sanitizer handy.

6. Pain Relievers and Medications

- Description: Be sure to pack any necessary medications, as well as over-the-counter pain relievers for headaches or sore muscles after a long day of walking.

Travel Essentials

1. Passport and Travel Documents

- Description: Keep your passport, travel insurance, and any other important documents in a safe and accessible place.

2. Travel Adapter

- Description: Germany uses Type C and F plugs with a standard voltage of 230V. Bring a travel adapter to charge your electronics.

3. Maps and Guidebooks
- Description: While most things can be accessed online, having a physical map or guidebook can be a lifesaver when your phone dies or there's no service.

4. Snacks
- Description: Bring along a few snacks like granola bars or nuts to keep your energy up while exploring.

5. Camera
- Description: If you want to capture high-quality photos of the market, consider bringing a compact camera along with your phone.

Optional Extras

1. Hot Water Bottle
- Description: A hot water bottle can be a comforting way to warm up after a day in the cold. Some accommodations provide them, but it's always nice to have your own.

2. Travel Blanket
- Description: A compact, foldable travel blanket can be useful for extra warmth on cold trains or in your hotel room.

3. Earplugs and Sleep Mask
- Description: If you're staying in a bustling city, earplugs and a sleep mask can help you get a good night's rest despite the festive noise.

By packing these essentials, you'll be well-prepared for a cozy and enjoyable experience at Germany's

Christmas markets. Remember to leave a little extra room in your suitcase for souvenirs and treats you'll pick up along the way!

GERMAN CHRISTMAS MARKET ETIQUETTE AND CULTURAL TIPS

Christmas markets in Germany are cherished traditions with deep cultural roots. To ensure that you have an enjoyable and respectful experience, it's important to understand the local customs and etiquette. Here are some key guidelines for visiting German Christmas markets, helping you navigate the festive atmosphere with confidence and courtesy.

General Etiquette

1. Greet and Thank Vendors
- Tip: When approaching a vendor, greet them with a simple "Guten Tag" (Good day) or "Frohe Weihnachten" (Merry Christmas). After your

transaction, be sure to thank them with "Danke schön" (Thank you very much). Politeness is highly valued in Germany, and acknowledging vendors with a greeting and thanks is considered courteous.

2. Respect Personal Space
- Tip: German markets can get crowded, especially in the evening. While enjoying the festivities, be mindful of personal space and avoid pushing through crowds. If you accidentally bump into someone, a quick "Entschuldigung" (Excuse me) is appreciated.

3. Keep the Markets Clean
- Tip: Germany prides itself on cleanliness, and this extends to its Christmas markets. Dispose of trash properly and return any reusable cups, mugs, or plates to the vendors. Most markets have designated recycling bins, so be sure to use them.

4. Be Mindful of Photography

- Tip: While it's tempting to capture every beautiful stall and festive decoration, be mindful when taking photos of people. Avoid photographing vendors without their permission, and be respectful of other visitors who may not want to be in your shots.

5. Respect Local Traditions
- Tip: Christmas markets often have religious and cultural traditions that are important to locals. For example, you may encounter carolers or nativity scenes. It's important to show respect during these moments, even if you do not participate.

Food and Drink Etiquette

1. Enjoying Glühwein
- Tip: Glühwein (mulled wine) is a staple at German Christmas markets. When you order Glühwein, you'll often receive it in a decorative mug, which you can either return for a deposit refund or keep as a souvenir.

If you choose to keep the mug, let the vendor know and pay the extra fee. It's also considered polite to enjoy your drink near the stall rather than walking around with it, especially during peak times.

2. Sharing Tables
- Tip: At busy times, it's common for strangers to share tables, especially at food stalls. If you see an open seat at a communal table, politely ask "Ist dieser Platz noch frei?" (Is this seat taken?) before sitting down. Germans are generally open to sharing tables, as long as it's done respectfully.

3. Sampling and Ordering Food
- Tip: Christmas markets offer a variety of traditional German foods, from bratwurst to gingerbread. It's customary to wait patiently in line and avoid cutting in. If you're unsure about a particular dish, politely ask the vendor for a small sample. Most vendors are happy to let you try before you buy.

Cultural Norms

1. Punctuality
- Tip: Germans value punctuality, and this extends to Christmas markets. Many events, such as concerts or performances, start promptly at the scheduled time. Arriving early ensures you get a good spot, especially for popular events like the lighting of the Christmas tree or special performances.

2. Quiet Hours
- Tip: Even during the festive season, Germans observe quiet hours, particularly in residential areas. These hours usually start around 10 PM, so if you're staying near a market, be mindful of noise levels when returning to your accommodation late at night.

3. Tipping
- Tip: Tipping at Christmas markets is not mandatory but is appreciated, especially if you've received

exceptional service. A small tip of 5-10% is generally sufficient, and it's usually given directly to the vendor.

4. Dress Modestly

- Tip: While the Christmas markets are festive, they are also family-oriented and traditional. Dress warmly and modestly, avoiding overly revealing outfits. Germans tend to dress in a more subdued and practical manner during winter, so comfortable, layered clothing is recommended.

Safety and Security

1. Beware of Pickpockets

- Tip: Christmas markets can be crowded, making them a prime spot for pickpockets. Keep your valuables secure, preferably in a crossbody bag with zippers. Avoid keeping your wallet or phone in your back pocket, and always be aware of your surroundings.

2. Know Emergency Numbers

- Tip: In case of an emergency, it's important to know the local emergency numbers. The general emergency number in Germany is 112, which can be used for police, fire, or medical emergencies. Most markets also have security personnel on-site, so don't hesitate to approach them if you need assistance.

3. Stay Warm and Hydrated

- Tip: Spending long hours in cold weather can take a toll on your body. Dress in layers, take breaks indoors to warm up, and stay hydrated. Hot drinks like tea or hot chocolate can help, but don't forget to drink water as well.

Understanding the Local Culture

1. Embrace the Christmas Spirit

- Tip: German Christmas markets are about more than just shopping; they're a celebration of the holiday season. Take the time to enjoy the festive atmosphere, listen to live music, and participate in local traditions. Whether it's singing along to carols or watching a Christmas pageant, embracing the Christmas spirit will enhance your experience.

2. Be Patient

- Tip: Christmas markets are incredibly popular, and lines can get long, especially for food and drink. Patience is key to enjoying the experience without frustration. Take this time to soak in the surroundings and chat with fellow visitors.

3. Learn Basic German Phrases

- Tip: While many vendors speak English, learning a few basic German phrases can go a long way in showing respect for the local culture. Simple greetings like "Guten Tag" (Good day) and "Frohe Weihnachten" (Merry Christmas) will be appreciated, as well as polite expressions like "Bitte" (Please) and "Danke" (Thank you).

By following these etiquette guidelines and cultural tips, you'll not only have a more enjoyable experience at the German Christmas markets but also connect more deeply with the local traditions and festive spirit. The Christmas market season is a time of joy, togetherness, and celebration, and understanding the customs will help you make the most of this magical time in Germany.

USEFUL GERMAN PHRASES FOR HOLIDAY TRAVELERS

When traveling in Germany, especially during the holiday season, having a basic understanding of the language can make a significant difference in your experience. While many Germans speak English, knowing a few key phrases can help you navigate your way through daily interactions and enhance your cultural immersion. Below is a collection of useful German phrases for holiday travelers, complete with their meanings and pronunciations.

Greetings and Polite Expressions

- Guten Tag (goo-ten tahg) – Good day

- Hallo (hah-loh) – Hello

- Guten Morgen (goo-ten mor-gen) – Good morning

- Guten Abend (goo-ten ah-bent) – Good evening

- Gute Nacht (goo-teh nahkt) – Good night

- Wie geht's? (vee gates) – How are you?

- Mir geht es gut (meer gate es goot) – I am fine

- Danke (dahn-kuh) – Thank you

- Bitte (bit-teh) – Please / You're welcome

- Entschuldigung (ent-shool-dee-goong) – Excuse me / I'm sorry

- Prost! (prohst) – Cheers!

Greeting someone politely is a great way to start a conversation, and it can also help you make a positive impression. Germans appreciate good manners, so learning these greetings is essential.

Shopping and Dining

- Ich hätte gern... (ikh heh-teh gehrn) – I would like...

- Könnte ich die Speisekarte sehen? (kurn-teh ikh dee shpy-ze-kar-teh zay-en) – Could I see the menu?

- Was empfehlen Sie? (vahs empfay-len zee) – What do you recommend?

- Ich bin Vegetarier/in (ikh bin veh-ge-tah-ree-er/een) – I am a vegetarian (add "in" if you are female)

- Wo ist die Toilette? (voh ist dee toy-let-teh) – Where is the bathroom?

- Wie viel kostet das? (vee feel kost-et dahs) – How much does that cost?

- Könnte ich bitte die Rechnung haben? (kurn-teh ikh bit-teh dee rey-khnoong hah-ben) – Could I have the bill, please?

These phrases will be especially useful when dining in restaurants or shopping for souvenirs and gifts. The ability to ask for a menu, request the bill, or inquire about prices in German will make your holiday experience smoother.

Travel and Directions

- Wo ist…? (voh ist) – Where is…?

  - Example: Wo ist der Bahnhof? (voh ist der bahn-hof) – Where is the train station?

- Wie komme ich zu…? (vee kom-meh ikh tsoo) – How do I get to…?

  - Example: Wie komme ich zum Flughafen? (vee kom-meh ikh tsoom floog-hah-fen) – How do I get to the airport?

- Ich habe mich verlaufen (ikh hah-beh mikh fer-lau-fen) – I am lost

- Könnten Sie mir helfen? (kurn-ten zee meer hel-fen) – Could you help me?

- Welches Gleis? (vel-khes glyce) – Which platform?

- Wann fährt der Zug ab? (vahn fehrt der tsoog ahb) –
When does the train leave?

When navigating Germany's efficient public transportation system, these phrases will be indispensable. Asking for directions, finding the right platform, or inquiring about departure times can make your journey hassle-free.

Accommodations and Emergencies

- Haben Sie ein Zimmer frei? (hah-ben zee ine tseem-mer fry) – Do you have a room available?
- Ich habe eine Reservierung (ikh hah-beh ine re-zer-vee-roong) – I have a reservation
- Ich brauche Hilfe (ikh brow-khe hil-feh) – I need help
- Rufen Sie die Polizei! (roo-fen zee dee poh-lie-tsye) – Call the police!
- Wo ist das nächste Krankenhaus? (voh ist dahs naekh-steh krahn-ken-house) – Where is the nearest hospital?

These phrases are vital in case of emergencies or when you need assistance at your hotel. Being able to ask for help or medical attention in German can be crucial in difficult situations.

Holiday and Festive Phrases

- Frohe Weihnachten (froh-heh vy-nahk-ten) – Merry Christmas
- Frohes neues Jahr (froh-es no-yess yahr) – Happy New Year
- Schöne Feiertage (shur-neh fy-er-tah-ge) – Happy Holidays
- Guten Rutsch! (goo-ten rootsh) – Happy New Year! (Literally, "Good slide" into the new year)

During the holiday season, these festive phrases will come in handy when greeting people or enjoying the Christmas markets and seasonal events.

Basic Numbers

- Eins (ine-s) – One

- Zwei (tsvy) – Two

- Drei (dry) – Three

- Vier (feer) – Four

- Fünf (fuen-f) – Five

- Sechs (zecks) – Six

- Sieben (zee-ben) – Seven

- Acht (ahkht) – Eight

- Neun (noyn) – Nine

- Zehn (tsayn) – Ten

Learning numbers can be especially helpful when shopping, asking for directions, or booking tickets.

By learning these basic phrases, you can make your holiday in Germany more enjoyable, less stressful, and more immersive. While Germans are known for their proficiency in English, showing an effort to speak their language is often appreciated and can lead to a richer travel experience.

Winter travel in Germany can be magical, with picturesque snowy landscapes, festive Christmas markets, and cozy alpine retreats. However, it also comes with its own set of challenges, from icy roads to unpredictable weather conditions. Being well-prepared for winter travel is essential for staying safe and making the most of your holiday adventure. Below are key safety tips and emergency contacts to ensure a worry-free winter journey in Germany.

Weather Awareness and Preparation

Germany's winter weather can range from mild to harsh, with snow, ice, and cold temperatures common, especially in mountainous regions. It's crucial to stay informed about the weather conditions during your travels.

- Check the Forecast: Regularly check weather reports through apps like WetterOnline or Deutscher Wetterdienst (DWD) for real-time updates.
- Dress Warmly: Layer your clothing to stay warm and dry. A good winter coat, waterproof boots, gloves, a scarf, and a hat are essential. Consider thermal underwear and wool socks for extra warmth.
- Carry Essentials: Keep a winter survival kit in your car or backpack, including items like a blanket, a flashlight, a first-aid kit, water, snacks, and a portable phone charger.

Staying warm and dry is crucial, as hypothermia and frostbite are real risks in cold environments. Make sure to pack appropriately for all outdoor activities.

Transportation Safety

Whether you're traveling by car, train, or plane, winter travel requires extra caution to ensure safety on the road and during your journey.

- Driving in Winter:

  - Ensure your vehicle is equipped with winter tires (mandatory in Germany during winter months).

  - Check your car's battery, windshield wipers, and antifreeze levels before driving.

  - Keep a safe distance from other vehicles, especially on icy roads, and drive at reduced speeds.

  - If you encounter black ice (Glätte), avoid sudden braking and steer gently.

- Public Transportation:

  - Allow extra time for potential delays due to snow or ice.

  - Be cautious on icy platforms at train stations and bus stops.

- Follow the safety instructions on public transport and be aware of emergency exits.

Public transportation in Germany is generally reliable, but winter weather can lead to delays, so planning ahead is vital.

Winter Sports and Outdoor Activities

Germany offers a range of winter sports activities, from skiing in the Alps to ice skating on frozen lakes. However, these activities come with inherent risks, and safety should always be a top priority.

- Skiing and Snowboarding:
  - Always wear a helmet and appropriate safety gear.
  - Check avalanche reports and be aware of marked trails.
  - Don't ski or snowboard alone, and keep within designated areas.

- Hiking and Snowshoeing:

  - Stick to well-marked paths and trails.

  - Bring a map, compass, or GPS device, and inform someone of your route before heading out.

  - Be prepared for sudden weather changes, and carry a survival kit including extra food, water, and warm clothing.

Outdoor winter activities are fun, but always respect the environment and your own limits. If conditions seem unsafe, it's better to delay or cancel your plans.

Health and Wellness

Cold weather can take a toll on your health, so it's essential to take care of yourself during your winter travels.

- Stay Hydrated: Cold weather can reduce your thirst, but staying hydrated is crucial for maintaining energy and preventing dehydration.

- Eat Warm, Nutritious Meals: Hot meals and drinks help keep your body temperature up. Enjoy hearty German winter foods like soups, stews, and roasted meats.

- Take Breaks: If you're spending long periods outside, take regular breaks indoors to warm up and rest.

Taking care of your physical well-being can help prevent common winter ailments like colds and flu.

Emergency Contacts and Procedures

In case of emergencies, it's important to know the local emergency numbers and have access to essential contacts.

- Emergency Numbers:

  - 112: The general European emergency number for fire, police, and ambulance services.

- 110: Direct line to the police in Germany.

- Medical Assistance:

- Ärztlicher Bereitschaftsdienst (116 117): This is the number for the on-call medical service in Germany. You can call it for non-life-threatening medical issues.

- Local Hospitals: Know the location of the nearest hospital or medical facility in case of illness or injury.

- Embassy Contacts:

- Keep the contact information of your country's embassy in Germany. In case of lost documents, legal trouble, or other major issues, your embassy can provide crucial assistance.

- Insurance Coverage: Make sure you have adequate travel insurance that covers medical emergencies, winter sports, and cancellations due to weather-related disruptions.

Having these emergency contacts and procedures at your fingertips can provide peace of mind during your travels.

Winter Travel Etiquette and Local Laws

Germany has specific laws and etiquette when it comes to winter safety, and understanding them can help you avoid any legal issues.

- Sidewalk Clearing: In many parts of Germany, property owners are responsible for clearing snow and ice from sidewalks in front of their homes or businesses. Be mindful of this responsibility if you are staying in a rental property.

- Winter Tire Law: As mentioned earlier, winter tires are mandatory in winter conditions. Failing to comply can result in fines, and insurance may not cover accidents if your car isn't properly equipped.

Following local regulations and respecting winter travel etiquette helps ensure a smooth and enjoyable holiday experience.

Traveling in Germany during the winter holidays offers an enchanting experience filled with festive markets, snow-covered landscapes, and cozy moments. However, the season also presents unique challenges, and being well-prepared is key to staying safe and making the most of your winter adventure. By following these safety tips and keeping emergency contacts handy, you can enjoy a worry-free holiday in Germany, surrounded by the beauty and magic of the season.

NOTE
(Write Your Experience Here!)

....

....

....

....

....

....

....

....

....

....

....

....

....

....

....

....

....

Merry Christmas &
Happy New Year!

Made in United States
Troutdale, OR
10/19/2024

23903551R00106